# Consumption Matters

D0755595

# Consumption Matters
## A Psychological Perspective

Cathrine Jansson-Boyd
*Senior Lecturer, Anglia Ruskin University, UK*

palgrave
macmillan

First published 2011 by
PALGRAVE MACMILLAN

Palgrave Macmillan in the UK is an imprint of Macmillan Publishers Limited, registered in England, company number 785998, of Houndmills, Basingstoke, Hampshire RG21 6XS.

Palgrave Macmillan in the US is a division of St Martin's Press LLC, 175 Fifth Avenue, New York, NY 10010.

Palgrave Macmillan is the global academic imprint of the above companies and has companies and representatives throughout the world.

Palgrave® and Macmillan® are registered trademarks in the United States, the United Kingdom, Europe and other countries.

ISBN: 978–0–230–20117–0

This book is printed on paper suitable for recycling and made from fully managed and sustained forest sources. Logging, pulping and manufacturing processes are expected to conform to the environmental regulations of the country of origin.

A catalogue record for this book is available from the British Library.

Library of Congress Cataloging-in-Publication Data

Jansson-Boyd, Cathrine V.
    Consumption matters : a psychological perspective / Cathrine Jansson-Boyd.
        p. cm.
    Includes index.
    Summary: "Can shopping make you happy? How do the things you consume mould your identity? Jansson-Boyd provides an engaging and lively introduction to consumer issues that encompasses shopping, the influence of the media, the environment and more. The book will interest readers that have questioned how living in a consumer society affects human behaviour"—Provided by publisher.
    ISBN 978–0–230–20117–0 (pbk.)
    1. Consumer behavior—Psychological aspects. 2. Shopping—Social aspects. 3. Shopping—Psychological aspects. 4. Shopping—Environmental aspects. 5. Shopping—Moral and ethical aspects. I. Title.
HF5415.32.J36 2011
306.3—dc23                                    2011024443

10  9  8  7  6  5  4  3  2  1
20  19  18  17  16  15  14  13  12  11
Printed in China

# Contents

v

# Illustrations

## Table

## Figures

# Acknowledgements

I am especially grateful to Alexander for all the support he has given me whilst writing this book. Without his support this book might never have materialised. Undoubtedly he is my one true rock.

Thank you to those who have granted me permission to reprint images. The book would not be the same without them.

I would also like to thank the team at Palgrave Macmillan for their constructive comments and encouragement.

# Introduction

Consumption affects everybody around the globe, whether directly or indirectly. It is particularly evident in Westernised, industrialised societies where shopping is often at the heart of the economy. The fact that it affects the entire population ought to mean that each and every one of us should be interested in knowing how it impacts upon us. Unfortunately, this is often not the case, especially when it comes to psychologists. It appears that consumer matters are often deemed to be something frivolous and much less important than other scientific areas. Failing to see how the consumer society affects people's mental health, physical health, attitudes, moral reasoning, identity and happiness is a failure to understand human beings. Luckily, the interest in consumer-related matters is growing and it appears that more and more scientists are opening up to the fact that consumer-related issues are an integral part of understanding humans.

When discussing what it means to live in a consumer society and why consumption matters, one should recognise that it is not just about the kinds of products that consumers buy. Instead there are many other issues that need to be taken into consideration when discussing the importance of consumption. Consumers no longer only consume products and services; they are also consuming people and the environment.

## Constant pressure to consume

One of the reasons why it is important to understand consumer issues is because people are often pressured to consume. This may at times be an explicit pressure but more often it is an implicit one. That large companies are trying to persuade people to consume is evident from the hundreds of thousands of advertising messages that we are continuously exposed to and in how the films and

television programmes that we watch for entertainment are suf-
fused with product placements. Because the survival of companies
depends on consumers buying what they are selling (Korten, 1995),
they make use of marketing techniques that aim to make people
think that their products can improve their lives (e.g. Herman &
Chomsky, 1988; Klein, 1999).

The pressure to consume is largely created by huge, powerful
corporations whose sole aim is to make money. However, people
are also encouraged indirectly by the individualistic culture that
is a big part of Westernised and industrialised societies. Western
societies have for a long time encouraged people to stand on
their own two feet and on occasion politicians have made it clear
that people have to fend for themselves. This was particularly
obvious when Margaret Thatcher declared: 'There is no such
thing as society. There are individual men and women and there
are families' (1987, cited in Kingdom, 1992). Such comments
clearly underline the Western philosophy that it is important to
be individualistic.

In most Western countries people are socialised into believing that qualities such as initiative, independence, boldness,
self-reliance and self-responsibility are highly valued (Keat,
1991). Because of the continuous encouragement from society
that people need to be individualistic, people often try to define
themselves through consumption (see Chapter 2 for further
information). It may seem paradoxical that individuals rely on
consuming the right products and services in order to show the
rest of the world that they are individualistic, especially since the
majority of the products they purchase are mass manufactured,
meaning that there will be millions of people all owning identical products.

The constant pressure to consume often moulds people into being
something that may not necessarily represent their true selves. It
is very difficult for individuals to resist being swept away by the
strong consumer tide. When people think that they have managed
to remain unaffected by the consumer culture, it may be because
they fail to realise the true impact it has on them. Often people
forget that things such as taking a walk in a park, heating up the
house, going on holiday and buying plants for the garden, all count
as consumer activities and all affect us, and sometimes others, in
ways we may not have thought about.

## The aim of this book

The purpose of this book is to present the reader with different types of consumer activities that affect people as well as the environment in which we live. It is hoped that a clear picture will emerge so that it becomes evident how consumption is an important part of people's lives and how it impacts on human behaviour and psychological well-being. This book should be of interest to anybody who wishes to learn about the psychology of consumption.

It is beyond the scope of this book to present an in-depth picture of all the different aspects of consumption, and there are a lot of other factors that may be highly relevant even though they are not mentioned here. Whilst writing this book, I discussed the content with many colleagues and all had slightly different ideas in regard to what should be in the book and what should be the emphasis of each chapter. It is simply not possible to include everything related to consumption and psychology. This book has been written in the hope that it will be an enjoyable read that can be read at any time and in any place, and not a tome that just sits on the bookshelf and collects dust.

Rather than incorporating too much into the one book I am urging readers to explore the area of consumption further. The subject is undeniably a fascinating one and I suspect that it is never possible to learn too much about it.

## Content

The book is divided into seven freestanding chapters and each one looks at a particular topic that is important when it comes to understanding why consumption matters. Each chapter presents key research findings within its area but does not necessarily provide the reader with all the answers. Instead it is left open for you to draw your own conclusions from what you have read. Naturally, as with any area of psychology, there may be certain aspects in the book that connect the chapters in some way. However, all the chapters in this book examine different topics within the consumer area and are therefore probably best treated as separate.

The first chapter in this book provides an overview of how the consumer culture plays a part in children's lives. It presents an overview of topics such as how television can cause children to get a skewed picture of the world and whether exposure to television violence has a detrimental impact on their behaviour and well-being. The chapter also looks at the role of computer games in children's lives. Additionally, this chapter also examines how a constant stream of food advertisements may contribute to the fact that children are becoming increasingly overweight.

Chapter 2 outlines how material possessions are used to create people's identities as well as to inform others about who they are. It also explores where the 'meaning' of products comes from and how such meaning can be used to signify group membership. The chapter then goes on to look at the intertwined relationship between group membership, identity and consumption. Finally the chapter outlines three aspects that can be obstacles when trying to establish an identity within the consumer society.

In Chapter 3 the focus turns to how consumption is detrimental to the environment. The aim of this chapter is to show that the true cost of consumption is not always included in the price that consumers pay. Bearing in mind that if the planet's entire 6 billion population were to enjoy the same consumption patterns as those in the Western societies, three more planet Earths would be needed (Porritt, 2004), it is easy to understand that the link between consumption and our environment needs to be taken seriously.

The fourth chapter deals with two particular ethical issues: human rights and animal welfare. First, the chapter outlines human rights issues such as fair pay and exploitation of child workers. It also outlines specific aspects of animal welfare, including treatment of livestock and cosmetic testing on animals. How consumers think and behave in regard to unethical practices is dealt with next and the chapter concludes by asking who should be held responsible for unethical consumption.

Chapter 5 focuses on the link between the consumer society and people's physical appearance. It specifically looks at how body appearance can be linked to the media. In the case of obesity it is possible that repeated exposures to advertisements for foods high in fat content are at least partially to blame (e.g. Crespo et al., 2001). The media may also be responsible for people believing that they have to be thin in order to be beautiful (e.g. Thompson, Kent, & Smith, 2002). This chapter also takes a look at why it is increasingly common for individuals to turn to cosmetic surgery.

Consumption as a means to happiness is the topic of Chapter 6. It explores whether consumer activities have the capacity to make people happy. In order to address this, a range of topics such as how people become materialistic and what it means to have materialistic value orientations are discussed. Furthermore, different approaches to consumption are outlined in order to shed some light on whether consumption is synonymous with being unhappy. The final section of the chapter presents some ideas in regard to what people should consume if they wish to feel overall more satisfied.

The final chapter is about how damaging consumption can be for people's well-being if they become addicted to material possessions. This may be in the form of being a compulsive shopper or a hoarder. Both disorders, to some extent, resemble obsessive-compulsive disorder (e.g. Christenson et al., 1994). The emphasis is mainly on compulsive buyers and aspects such as why they become addicted, the kind of difficulties they are faced with and how they can be treated are all looked at.

At the end of each chapter a 'real life' example of a particular issue is covered, which is followed by a couple of questions you may wish to try to answer, and then finally there are recommendations of additional materials that may be of interest to you. The recommended additional materials have been divided into three categories: reading, films and useful websites. By covering three types of media it is hoped that something will appeal to you so that you feel inspired to explore the areas covered in this book further.

# I

# Young Consumers: Are They the Beauty and the Consumer Society the Beast?

Manufacturers know that it can be lucrative to aim their products and services at young consumers. The toy industry alone is worth an estimated £2 billion in the UK (British Toy and Hobby Association, 2007), whilst in the US it is worth a staggering $22 billion (All Business, 2007). Let's not forget that children also consume a high amount of other products such as books, clothes, music, sweets, shoes and mobile phones.

If children themselves do not have the money to spend, they most certainly have the capacity to persuade their parents to buy products and services for them (Greenberg, Fazel, & Weber, 1986; Tinsley, 2002), making them a consumer force to be reckoned with.

From the moment children are born they are caught up in a whirlwind of messages to consume, which socialises them into becoming 'good consumers' for life (Chandler & Heinzerling, 1999). At an early age they become avid consumers of television, the Internet, magazines, films and computer games (e.g. Brown, Childers, Bauman, & Koch, 1990; Larson & Verma, 1999). Estimates suggest that children spend somewhere between 2 and 5 hours in front of a television or a computer screen and around

5 hours listening to the radio or alternative audio equipment, on a daily basis (Brown et al., 1990; Larson & Verma, 1999; Ofcom, 2007; Roberts, Foehr, Rideout, & Brodie, 1999).

## Square eyes

Some children spend more time watching television than they do at school (Lloyd-Kolkin, 1982)! It is well documented that children in Western countries, in particular, watch a lot of television and that such viewing averages 15 hours a week (Beentjes, Koolstra, Marseille, & van der Voort, 2001). Such extensive viewing has been found to be applicable to most age groups (e.g. Bernard-Bonnin, Gilbert, Rousseau, Masson, & Maheux, 1991; Owens et al., 1999), although children under the age of 6 watch a little less, around 6–9 hours a week (Vandewater, Bickham, Lee, Cummings, Wartella, & Rideout, 2005). However, these figures do not include secondary TV viewing (viewing that accompanies another activity). Secondary viewing has been found to be prevalent among children and estimates suggest that it adds another 1.5 hours a week of television viewing for 3–5-year-olds (Wright et al., 2001). Additionally, it has been found that approximately 35% of children live in a home where the television is on most of the time (Vandewater et al., 2005).

Through television (as well as other media sources) children learn about the world in general (Clifford, Gunter, & McAleer, 1995) and it also shapes them as individuals (e.g. Comstock, 1991; Strasburger & Wilson, 2002). Consequently, it is important to be aware how different types of television programmes affect children.

## Excessive television watching and adult programmes

Several studies have identified general consequences of watching too much television (including children's programmes). For example, it has been found that children lose their creative flair and as a result find it difficult to keep themselves entertained without a television (Kubey, 1986). Additionally, those who view too many general-audience programmes can become less adequate readers

(Koolstra, van der Voort, & van der Kamp, 1997) and poorer performers on cognitive tests (Wright et al., 2001). Hence letting children overindulge in programmes such as *Friends*, *One Tree Hill*, or *Eastenders* is not going to aid their academic performance. The fact that general-audience programmes have been found to impact detrimentally on children shows that some are watching television that is aimed at adults.

In some countries there are as many as 25 channels specifically aimed at children (Ofcom, 2007), giving young people plenty of choice in regard to what they watch. Even with a high number of programmes and channels intended for children, their viewing is by no means restricted to those channels. These days most children have a television in their room, meaning that parents often can't control what they watch on TV and for how long (Ofcom, 2007). Letting children control their television viewing is not ideal (American Academy of Pediatrics Committee on Public Education, 2001; Strasburger, 1992) as they are unaware of the potential consequences (Jason & Hanaway, 1997). The drawbacks of children watching adult programming include sleep disturbances and decreased sleep length (Paavonen, Pennonen, Roine, Valkonen, & Lahikainen, 2006). Another potential problem is the early onset of sexual activity amongst teens. A longitudinal study conducted by the Children's Hospital in Boston, US, where children were tracked from age 6 to 18, found that the younger a child is when they are exposed to television content intended for adults, the earlier they become sexually active during adolescence (Science Daily, 2009).

## Consequences of a steady diet of violence

Another factor that also has an adverse effect upon children is exposure to violence in the media. Somewhere in the region of 40% of all children's television programmes shown contain acts of violence (Gunter & Harrison, 1997), a figure that is now likely to be considerably higher. Even children's cartoons such as *Tom and Jerry* have a high number of violent scenes in them (Gerbner, 1972).

It has been estimated that a child that is brought up in a Westernised society is likely to have seen over 8,000 murders and over 100,000 violent acts by late childhood (Bushman & Anderson, 2001). If children also watch cable TV and play

computer games, the numbers of violent acts they are exposed
to are likely to be even higher, since such media often contains
even more violence (Subrahmanyam, Kraut, Greenfield, & Gross,
2001). With every violent act children are exposed to they gradually become more accustomed to it, and they eventually think
nothing of it and do not respond to seeing violence, whether it is
on screen or in real life (Holland, 2000; Rule & Ferguson, 1986).
Even though a programme such as *Tom and Jerry* may seem
harmless, it allows children to become gradually accustomed to
onscreen violence.

Children that are fed a steady diet of media violence often genuinely do not understand what they have seen. Because they have
not fully developed moral understanding (e.g. Kohlberg, 1981;
Piaget, 1948; Potter, 1998) and the ability to process complex
information (e.g. Condry & Freund, 1989; Wright & Huston,
1983), they often misinterpret the information they encounter
(e.g. Flavell, Flavell, Green, & Korfmacher, 1990; Jaglom &
Gardner, 1981). The younger they are, the harder it is for them
to deal with the ramifications of violence and understand that
what they have seen is not real life (Bushman & Huesmann,
2001). Children's lack of life experience further complicates the
situation as it makes them very impressionable and consequently
more likely to imitate and replicate the behaviour they have seen
(Bandura, 1986, 2002).

It is unfortunate that few programmes show the consequences
of violence (Schechter, 2000) as children are less likely to imitate
aggressive behaviour if they see that you can get punished for it
(Bandura, 1986). Instead many programmes portray the bad guys
as being resourceful as well as successful (Dominick & Greenberg,
1972).

Children's lack of ability to fully process the information encountered coupled with their receptive nature may partially explain
why the media has been blamed for some heinous crimes committed by children. For example, in 1993, when two 11-year-old boys,
Jon Venables and Robert Thompson, were convicted of murdering
a 2-year-old boy in the UK, the judge said that he thought their
exposure to violent films might help explain why they had done
it. In the case of Jon Venables and Robert Thompson it has been
suggested that they were inspired by a film called *Child's Play 3*.
However, nobody knows for certain if this is true.

There are those who feel that the relationship between children and media violence is so apparent that perhaps there ought to be a ban on violent material (Newson, 1994). However, it is impossible to blame the media alone for such atrocious acts and it would be foolish to exclude other sources from which the tendency for violence may be derived, such as parents, siblings, school, or peers.

Most scientists generally accept that watching television violence can have a detrimental impact upon children. Even so there are those who claim that television violence does not affect children negatively. This being because children tend to forget what they have watched the evening before. If they can't remember what they have seen then how can it affect them? Additionally, it has been suggested that the more programmes children watch, the less specific are the details that they remember (Cullingford, 1984).

Nevertheless, the reality of exposing children to media violence was made clear in a joint statement issued by the American Academy of Pediatrics, the American Medical Association, the American Academy of Child and Adolescent Psychiatry and the American Psychological Association. Their shared opinion is that children are more likely to think that violence is acceptable, to resort to it when confronted with a difficult situation, and to be less inclined to help a person being attacked (American Academy of Pediatrics, 2000). That is not to say that they are suggesting that all children who are exposed to media violence become aggressive and will engage in anti-social behaviours. It simply increases the likelihood of such behaviours occurring.

## Learning to categorise people and objects

A high proportion of TV programmes make use of stereotypes, in regard to different countries, cultures and religions, criminals, men and women, which is something that children readily absorb (e.g. Clifford et al., 1995). It is understandable why children make use of what they have seen on television as it helps them get to grips with different types of people they may never meet. In particular, children's attitudes towards minority groups are often based upon what they have seen on the small screen (Berry, 2000). Minority groups such as Chinese, Africans and Asians are not commonly represented on television, and when they are, they are often segregated from whites and not always presented in a realistic manner (e.g. Taylor & Stern, 1997), leaving children to get a skewed picture of what they are like.

That children make use of the stereotypical information they have encountered through the media was particularly prominent in a study conducted by Holloway and Valentine in 2000. They asked 13-year-old British and New Zealand children to send descriptions via email of what they thought the people in the other country were like. Both groups of children referred to programmes and films they had seen to describe what the other nation was like. This demonstrates that when children have no first-hand experience of what other people are like they will make use of what they have come across in the media.

Other stereotypes they are likely to pick up on are specific behaviours that the media portray as being acceptable for men and women. Television is one of the main contributing factors in moulding humanity's understanding of gender roles (e.g. Durkin, 1985; Witt, 1997). Just like minority groups, men and women are not always accurately represented through the media. Men are generally overrepresented on television (McCauley, Thangavelu, & Rozin, 1988) and women are often portrayed as being less interesting. One such example can be noted from the *Spiderman* trilogy, whereby Peter Parker's girlfriend, Mary Jane Watson, is portrayed as a fragile individual who can't succeed in her chosen profession as an actress. She depends upon Spiderman to make her life exciting and she needs a male figure to look out for her.

Furthermore, older women are underrepresented, whilst men of all ages can be seen on our screens (e.g. Durkin, 1985; Kessler, Rakoczy, & Staudinger, 2004). How many films or programmes can you remember in which the leading role is played by a woman aged 40 or over? Most certainly you will be able to mention a few but the fact that women over 40 are underrepresented is something that is commonly debated amongst actors (Brown, 2009). The way in which women are presented contributes to stereotypical beliefs held by children (e.g. Durkin, 1985; Witt, 1997) and you may wish to consider the impact this may have upon young girls in particular.

## Underlying factors of excessive TV viewing

If parents knew *why* it is not good for their children to watch a lot of television, they might be more proactive in restricting the amount of time their children spend in front of the TV. Therefore educating parents properly on the influences of the media may help (American Academy of Pediatrics Committee on Public Education, 2001).

Other explanations for excessive television viewing have been linked to socio-economic factors. Children from low-income families have been found to spend a considerable amount of time in front of the television. So also do children who have mothers that have a low income and display maternal depressive symptoms (Conners, Tripathi, Clubb, & Bradley, 2007). Such findings indicate that parents might not always make a deliberate decision to let their child watch television. For example, it may be that parents in low-income families have to work extra long hours to support their family and consequently spend less time at home, meaning that they are unable to control exactly what their children are doing. The aforementioned research findings explain why some of the parents give their children free rein with respect to the television. However, there are bound to be plenty of additional explanations that are yet to be identified.

## What about watching pro-social behaviours on television?

Admittedly, there are more programmes on television containing aggressive and violent acts than there are those specifically showing pro-social behaviours. Nonetheless pro-social behaviours are shown on the small screen and research has found that children are actually more likely to imitate them than they are anti-social behaviours. Pro-social behaviours include a number of positive effects such as friendly interaction between individuals, learning, altruistic actions, safety activism and stereotype reduction (e.g. Hearold, 1986; Mares & Woodard, 2001). Programmes such as *Lassie* have been found to have a particularly positive impact on children.

Children are also likely to get a positive view of interracial attitudes if they are exposed to programmes, such as *Sesame Street*, where different nationalities are frequently featured (Greenfield, 1984). The very same programme has also been found to aid children's abilities to read and count (Rice, Huston, Truglio, & Wright, 1990; Zill, Davies, & Daly, 1994).

## Computer games

The use of computer games by children is a well researched and discussed area, just like television viewing. This is perhaps a natural development as computer games have increased in popularity amongst young individuals so much that they are now an established part of their everyday lives (e.g. Ferguson, 2010a; Greenberg, Sherry, Lachlan, Lucas, & Holmstrom, 2008; Roberts, Foehr, & Rideout, 2005).

One of the main concerns about playing computer games is that those who spend a lot of time playing them can become addicted. Addiction to computer games is now so prevalent in youths that as many as nearly 1 in 10 are thought to be pathological players (Gentile, 2009). This was found in a survey of 1,178 American youths aged 8–18. Those found to be pathological gamers played video games 24 hours per week, which was twice as much as non-addicted gamers. Additionally, the study found that being addicted to computer games was significantly linked to poorer school performance (Gentile, 2009). Addiction to computer games is now such a recognised problem that special clinics have been set up to treat those addicted to computer games (The Sunday Times, 2006).

One of the problems with pathological gamers is that they often withdraw from their social surroundings (Putnam, 2000). For children such withdrawal can lead to a breakdown in communication with their parents, something that may partially be caused by a parent's lack of understanding of computer games. The lack of understanding means that parents show no interest in the games that their children play and consequently children end up playing in isolation (Bonnafont, 1992, cited in Goldstein, 1994).

## Violent computer games

Another major concern in regard to computer games is the impact that violent games may have on children. The debate about violent computer games is very similar to that about violent television programmes in that some argue that violent computer games have a negative impact on children and others say that they don't. Undoubtedly the media has been (and still is) influential in the debates on violent games. The media has covered incidents such as the notorious Columbine High School shooting in 1999 with great gusto. The two teenagers involved in the shooting were said to have been inspired by a computer game called Doom (Glick et al., 1999) and just as in the case of Jon Venables and Robert Thompson, it is difficult to know what the underlying causes of their behaviour were. Because the media often whip up a storm about certain topics, it is essential not to get carried away with the emotions this may stir up. There is plenty of research that has investigated the impact of violent computer games upon children and it is perhaps not as clear cut as some would like it to be.

The idea that 'violence pays' is often evident in computer games in which being violent is the only way to win the game. Consequently some children may see aggressive acts as an acceptable tool to help them get what they want, a perception that will be further reinforced when they use aggression in real-life situations (Cole, Mills, Dale, & Jenkins, 1991). For example, if they push and shove other children to get to the head of a queue and the other children let them, this will be viewed as a positive outcome of being aggressive.

Some critics of violent media suggest that computer games are worse than television when it comes to affecting aggressive behaviours. This being due to the interactive nature of computer games, whereby players have to plan and perform the aggressive acts as opposed to simply watching them (e.g. Larson, 2001). The planning element is particularly applicable for online gaming as they need to carefully consider if they should and can take their opponent on.

If children get an inaccurate perception of violence by watching violent television and playing violent computer games, it is not difficult for parents to combat such views, even though it can be time consuming. A simple solution is to watch television and play computer games together with their children. Whilst doing so, parents can then explain to them that what they see does not portray real life and that violent behaviours are unacceptable (Collins, Sobol, & Westby, 1981). Children who have parents that do so have been found to be generally less aggressive (Singer, Singer, Desmond, Hirsch, & Nicol, 1998). However, due to life's many pressures it is not common parental practice (Huston & Wright, 1998).

## Are all gamers affected by violence?

Clearly not all children that play violent computer games show signs of aggression or violence. Bearing in mind that electronic games are now an everyday activity for most children (e.g. Greenberg et al., 2008; Roberts, Foehr et al., 2005), it can easily be observed that not all of them are behaving violently. Since the vast majority of gamers who play violent computer games do not engage in real-life violence it is important to address what kind of individuals are more likely to become affected by violent gaming (Markey & Markey, 2010). In instances such as the Columbine High School shooting, where the shooters were computer gamers (Anderson, 2004), it is important to note that they also possessed maladaptive characteristics (Markey & Markey, 2010). That may suggest that there are underlying personality traits that play a role in whether children choose to imitate violent computer games (Markey & Markey, 2010).

Psychoticism appears to be one personality trait that determines whether violent video games have a negative impact on the player. In a study conducted by Markey and Scherer (2009) it was found that those with high levels of psychoticism expressed more hostility and had higher levels of aggressive cognitions after being exposed to violent computer games. Perhaps unsurprisingly, research suggests that gamers with high levels of psychoticism experience less anxiety when killing a virtual computer character (Ravaja, Tupeinen, Saari, Puttonen, & Keltikangas-Jarvinen, 2008).

Another trait that can play a role in how people react to violent computer games is aggressiveness. Those who have high levels of trait aggressiveness are also often more hostile after playing violent games (Arriaga, Esteves, Carneiro, & Monteiro, 2006). Research on both aggressiveness and psychoticism may offer some form of explanation in regard to when and why violent computer games can have a detrimental effect on computer game players. The aforementioned is interesting in that it shows that there is still a lot to learn in regard to producing a clear picture of how violent computer games impact children.

## Propitious gaming

Not all research conducted on computer gaming is of a negative nature. Some statistics on children in Westernised countries appear to indicate that children who play computer games experience fewer behavioural problems than their non-playing counter-parts, and that they perform better on certain academic tests (e.g. Ferguson, 2010b). Hence, it is possible that the positive aspects of playing computer games may outweigh the previously identified negative aspects (Ferguson, 2010a).

Playing computer games can aid development of spatial perception and cognitive skills in young boys. Even relatively simple computer games such as Tetris have been found to improve mental rotation and spatial visualisation time on computer-based performance tests (Okagaki & Frensch, 1994). They also have the capacity to make children relax (Harris, 2001). Some have even gone as far as suggesting that we have computer games to thank for the increases in nonverbal and performance IQ scores (Greenfield, 1998) that we saw during the years when computer technology was becoming part of most people's lives (Flynn, 1994). The underlying reason for the increase in such scores is likely to be due to the fact that computer games can aid iconic representational skills (Greenfield, Brannon, & Lohr, 1994).

Perhaps a little more surprising is that violent computer games have been found to be more effective in improving cognitive abilities. Several studies have found that playing violent computer games is associated with higher visuospatial acuity, perception, processing, visual memory, and mental rotation (Castel, Pratt, & Drummond, 2005; Feng, Spence, & Pratt, 2007; Ferguson, Cruz, & Rueda, 2008; Green & Bavelier, 2003, 2007; Rosser et al., 2007). However, it is not clear why this is specific to violent computer games and why non-violent games produce weaker results (e.g. Quaiser-Pohl, Geiser, & Lehmann, 2006). Neither is it clear why non-gamers can't be trained to become just as good as expert gamers on visuospatial tasks (Boot, Kramer, Simons, Fabiani, & Gratton, 2008), indicating that there is still research to be conducted in order to fully understand the impact of computer games on cognition and behaviour.

The positive impact of playing violent games is not something that is commonly mentioned or written about (Ferguson, 2010b). One underlying reason for this and why violent computer games have gained such a bad reputation may be because some psychologists seem set on campaigning against them regardless of whether there are empirical data to support their detrimental claims (e.g.

Ferguson, 2010b; Gauntlett, 1995; Grimes, Anderson, & Bergen, 2008). Furthermore, the over-emphasis upon social learning is clearly evident in relation to how violent games affect people's behaviours (Ferguson, 2010b). This may be a problem since there are other factors, such as evolution and genes, that might explain people's aggressive and violent behaviours better than social influences (Ferguson, 2010c).

Finally, computers have also been found to be a useful tool for learning (e.g. Annetta, 2010). Having computers in the classroom has been shown to make the learning experience more enjoyable for children, as well as aid learning itself (e.g. Clements & Nastasi, 1992; Collis, 1996).

Research findings have also established that students who are taught to program a computer are likely to seek advice from other students when they are faced with a challenging task (Nastasi & Clements, 1993, 1994; Weinstein, 1991). Such findings show that if computers are used correctly in the classroom environment they are likely to aid overall learning and social interactions between the students.

Similar results have also been found for children who use computers at home. Rather than isolating them socially, the computers act as a tool to attract friends to play with (Crook, 1992).

## Why do children want to play computer games?

Children seem to want to play computer games for all sorts of reasons. Some of the less desirable research findings discussed earlier can also be partially contested by looking at the underlying motives for playing computer games.

In an extensive study where 1,254 children took part, a wide range of reasons were identified in regard to why children want to play computer games, as can be seen in Figure 1.1 (Olson et al., 2007). The study also identified that there were statistically significant differences between boys and girls in their underlying motivations for playing. For example, boys were more likely than girls to play for fun, for excitement, for the challenge of figuring the game out, to compete with others and to win.

There are also a number of different factors that have been identified in studies as being underlying reasons as to why children play computer games. Among these factors are that games provide

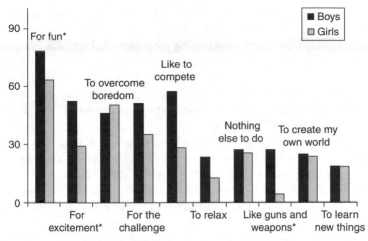

Figure 1.1   Motivations for computer game play

*Notes*: The figure shows the top 10 reasons why both boys and girls like to play computer games. Motivations followed by an asterisk (*) indicate that boys were statistically more likely to play for the given reason than girls.

*Source*: Adapted from Olson et al. (2007). Original graph from *Journal of Adolescent Health*, 41, 'Factors correlated with violent video game use by adolescent boys and girls', 77–83, Copyright Elsevier.

social interaction (Ito & Bittani, 2009), a topic of conversation (Olson, Kutner, & Warner, 2008), and an opportunity of doing things that they can't do in real life (Cragg, Taylor, & Toombs, 2007).

For young boys, playing computer games can also be one way of reinforcing their social identity, as being good at gaming is viewed as a highly desirable trait amongst peers (Tarrant et al., 2001) and can therefore increase their social status (e.g. Pellegrini, 2003). It is worth noting that the underlying motives for playing games are not consistent throughout childhood (Greenberg et al., 2008) and hence the desire to play may change with age.

## Commercial menus for children

Whilst watching television, browsing on the Internet, and reading magazines, children are constantly bombarded with messages encouraging them to buy various products and services. Such messages may appear in the form of product placement within a film or programme or through commercials. It is difficult to determine exactly how many advertising messages children are exposed to but estimates suggest that they see between 30,000 and 40,000 commercials on a yearly basis (Condry, Bence, & Scheibe, 1988; Kunkel & Gantz, 1992). That is not to say that they pay attention to all the advertising messages they encounter (Greer, Potts, Wright, & Huston, 1982).

Advertising aimed at children has been for a long time, and remains, a controversial area. Some countries have banned advertising for children as they deem it highly immoral to target individuals who do not always understand the meaning behind the message (e.g. Sweden, where advertising is not allowed for children aged below 12).

Generally children need to be aged 8 and above to be aware that the aim of advertising is to persuade people to buy things (Gaines & Esserman, 1981; Gunter, Oates, & Blades, 2005). Contrary to beliefs that those children who can state they have seen a commercial can also understand it, such assumptions have been found to be incorrect (Kunkel, 1988). Prior to 8, most children simply believe that they are informative and entertaining. Consequently, children often want what they have seen advertised (Isler, Popper, & Ward, 1987). The fact that children do not fully understand what they are exposed to makes them vulnerable to marketers' persuasive techniques and therefore it is not hard to present a product in a favourable light.

One commonly used technique is to try to create a 'happy brand personality' (Barcus, 1980; Kunkel & Gantz, 1992). Instead of making use of factual information in the adverts they use lots of images that are clearly associated with happiness. By repeated exposure to such images children eventually associate the brand with the 'happy images' and hence will perceive the brand as a happy one. A 'happy brand personality' is often achieved by making use of a 'spokes-character', such as Ronald McDonald or Kellogg's Tony the Tiger, that has the capacity to make young children laugh (Wartella & Hunter, 1983). Once children have a positive view of brands and products it can be difficult for guardians to explain potential problems with them, something that can become a problem when parents do not wish their children to have the products advertised.

## Overweight children

It is common that children ask their guardians specifically for foods that they have seen advertised (Jeffrey, McLellarn, & Fox, 1982; Taras, Sallis, Patterson, Nader, & Nelson, 1989). The majority of the advertising aimed at children advertises toys, cereal, sweets and fast food restaurants (Barcus, 1980; Kunkel & Gantz, 1992). In a society where obesity is increasingly a problem it is not helpful that a large proportion of adverts focus upon products that children can eat. Especially since most of those ads are for foods that have high contents of fat and sugar (Kotz & Story, 1994).

Between 16% and 18% of all the children in the UK are obese (The Information Centre, 2006), and approximately 25–33% of children in the US are obese or at risk of becoming seriously overweight (Kids Health, 2005; Troiano & Flegal, 1998). Researchers have found that there is a relationship between obesity and television watching (e.g. Crespo et al., 2001), and that the relationship becomes stronger as the amount of television watching increases (e.g. Dennison, Erb, & Jenkins, 2002). The relationship between television watching and obesity is further strengthened for children who belong to low-income families or those who have less educated parents (Kumanyika & Grier, 2006). Presumably the explanation lies in such children having access to more unhealthy snacks because they are generally cheaper to buy.

Not everybody is convinced that there is a link between obesity and television viewing as there are those who claim that such a relationship does not exist (e.g. DuRant, Baranowski, Johnson, & Thompson, 1994). Even though a number of recent findings suggest that there is a relationship, this is an area that can benefit from further research. It is possible that the correlation between television viewing and obesity is the result of sitting still in front of the small screen rather than engaging in physically demanding activities. A child that watches a lot of television will burn fewer calories than a child that is actively playing outside.

The media in particular has been keen to blame marketers and advertisers for child obesity because of their eagerness to advertise unhealthy food products to children (e.g. Carvel, 2006; McArdle, 2010). Marketers sometimes shield themselves by stating that they do incorporate messages such as 'should be consumed as part of a healthy diet' into the adverts, but research has found that children more often than not fail to understand such product disclosures (Liebert, Sprafkin, Liebert, & Rubinstein, 1977; Stern & Resnik, 1978). The result being that some children think that it is a great idea to eat Coco Pops for every meal, every day.

Although there appears to be a relationship between television watching, food commercials and obesity, it is not to say that junk food advertising is solely to blame for obesity problems in young children. There are numerous other factors that also play a part in why children put on a lot of weight. For example, it is known that children often model their own eating behaviour upon that of their parents (Ray & Klesges, 1993). Others suggest that it is partially or entirely due to our genes (e.g. Cardon, 1994), whilst some have identified education and income as contributing factors (Kumanyika, 1993).

## Making sense of consumption

Because little is written about the positive nature of consumption, it is easy to forget that consumption can also enrich children's lives. This chapter has addressed how a range of products and services can help children both academically and socially provided they are used in an appropriate way. Naturally, any activity that dwarfs a child's other educational or leisure activities is likely to have a detrimental effect upon the child's social and educational development (e.g. Griffiths, 1997), so the key is to ensure that consumption is well balanced.

Even though there are potential problems with children being brought up in a consumer society, it is probably not advisable to try to shelter them from it. Consumption is an integral part of human life, and if you try to protect some individuals from it, you are simply making them less equipped to deal with everyday life. For example, part of everyday life is exposure to violent images. News coverage includes pictures of dead bodies and people getting killed. Cinema posters plastered all over tube and train platforms show scenes of violence and blood. Advertising for the TV programme *CSI* recently made use of a picture where a body was lying in a large pool of blood, whilst a poster for a film called *The Kingdom* showed a war scene with a dead man lying on the ground. Both advertising campaigns were displayed at tube stations across London for young children to see. Hence, some exposure to media violence can make children desensitised (e.g. Drabman & Thomas, 1974) so that they can deal with the reality around them. That is not to say that parents should allow their children to watch highly inappropriate TV programmes or let them play adult-rated computer games. It is simply to suggest that a small appropriate dose of what is part of our everyday Westernised lives will enable children to deal with realities they are faced with on a daily basis.

There seems to be a wind of change in regard to how society views and treats consumption-related issues. Increasingly, we get to read about the possible impact of consumption on children in mainstream papers and magazines as well as hearing about it on the news. Global companies are also changing how they choose to represent themselves. Previously, Walt Disney was closely associated with McDonald's, through their 'Happy Meals' for children. However, in 2006 it was reported that they were to end their commercial venture. It did not appear to be a coincidence that the relationship ended at a time when obesity was frequently discussed in the media around the world, even though both firms denied that this was the underlying reason for their split.

The pressure of dealing with consumption is enormous for parents. It has both moral and financial implications for their lives. If children use computers to attract friends to play with them, then naturally a lot of parents are going to feel that their children should have a computer, something that a lot of families may not be able to afford. It is important that parents have a 'sober' view of what consumption is about, that they can see the positives as well as the negatives, so that they can deal with it effectively.

## Summary

Consumption is an integral part of children's lives. Too much television viewing can be unhealthy for children as it can affect how creative they are, their reading ability and cognitive performance. It can also impact how they view others. Violent television programmes can also have a detrimental effect on children in that they can make them desensitised and aggressive. However, watching television does not have to be bad. For example, pro-social programmes have the capacity to foster positive behaviours in young individuals. There are also other types of consumption that can have a positive influence on children such as using computers and playing computer games. Through television and other media children are bombarded with advertising messages, which they often fail to understand, making them vulnerable to their persuasive nature, which can lead to overconsumption.

### Blame it on the movie?

On 1 December 1997 a 14-year-old boy named Michael Carneal walked into a Kentucky high school dressed in black and shot eight students who were part of a small prayer group. Three of those students (Jessica James, Kayce Steger and Nicole Hadley) died and the remaining five were wounded. On the day of the shooting he had brought a pistol, two rifles, two shotguns and 700 rounds of ammunition, all of it stolen from a neighbour's garage. The young teenager was a year later sentenced to life in prison with possibility of parole after 25 years.

Michael was a freshman at the high school and was, according to reports, not fitting in well. He used to wear bright ill-fitting clothes and had occasional disciplinary problems. Apparently, his fellow students were not always very nice to him and there were rumours that he was bullied and suffered from depression. The headmaster for the high school said there had been no signs of violence in his background prior to the shooting and he had never been considered dangerous.

Close to the time of the shooting the 14-year-old had previously threatened to 'shoot up' the school, but the student he had mentioned it to thought that he was joking. Michael had been an avid computer user who logged onto Internet pornography sites to view sexually violent material. He also liked playing violent computer games such as Doom, Quake and Mortal Kombat. Since the young boy had never had any firearms training it was assumed that he had learned to shoot by playing the game Doom. In the game a gunman moves through buildings full of enemies. The aim is to shoot the enemies, and when they die they fall to the ground in pools of blood.

Carneal later admitted that he was also influenced by a film starring Leonardo DiCaprio called *The Basketball Diaries*, which contains a scene where the lead shoots his teacher and some of his classmates. It has been suggested that the shooting scene should be familiar even to those who have not seen the film simply because of the extensive coverage of the high school rampage.

Sometime after the shooting there was a failed attempt by the parents of Jessica James, Kayce Steger and Nicole Hadley to sue the makers of the video games and the movie that were suggested to have been liable for the school shooting. The court stated that the defendants could not possibly have foreseen how the products would have impacted the teenager.

## TO THINK ABOUT:

1. Should children be discouraged from consuming certain products and services?
2. Who is ultimately responsible for children's exposure to potentially harmful consumption such as violent television programmes or computer games?

## FURTHER READING THAT MAY BE OF INTEREST:

If you wish to read more about children as consumers, the following texts might be of interest.

- Roberts, D.F., & Foehr, U.G. (2004). *Kids & media in America.* Cambridge: Cambridge University Press.
- Pugh, A.J. (2009). *Longing and belonging: Parents, children, and consumer culture.* Berkeley: University of California Press.
- Mayo, E., & Nairn, A. (2009). *Consumer kids: How big business is grooming our children for profit.* London: Constable & Robinson.

## FILMS:

The Media Education Foundation has put together a film that looks at the commercialisation of childhood:
- *Consuming kids: The commercialization of childhood* (2008).

A full-length preview of the film can be seen online: http://www.mediaed.org/cgi-bin/commerce.cgi?preadd=action&key=134

## USEFUL WEBSITES:

To learn more about children and consumption you may find the following websites useful:

- **Global Issues:** http://www.globalissues.org/article/237/children-as-consumers
- **KidsHealth:** http://kidshealth.org/parent/positive/family/tv_affects_child.html
- **American Psychological Association:** http://www.apa.org/research/action/protect.aspx & http://www.apa.org/research/action/games.aspx

# 2

# Changing Our Identities by Changing Our Possessions

Prior to World War II people often defined who they were through their religious beliefs and their immediate and extended family. Our sense of self stemmed from core values and beliefs shared by small, close communities (e.g. Farr, 1996; Hogg & Williams, 2000; Wundt, 1916). In industrialised societies this is no longer the case. Fewer and fewer people are religious and long gone are small, close communities. People no longer believe in the same sort of things as they once did. The fact that people's belief systems have changed means that we have also changed the way we view ourselves. Such changes mean that people are often using material possessions — and consumer-related activities to construct or to reinforce their identities (Belk, 1988; Elliott & Wattanasuwan, 1998).

## Who am I?

If you were asked to describe who you are, you should be able to answer simple questions such as where you fit in and where you belong. There are numerous ways in which you may respond to a question that asks you to think of who you are. Telling people your name may be a natural response, or you may include what you do for a living and which country you are from (Belk, 2006). Whatever the answer, it should somehow be reflective of who you

are and the answer is also likely to differ depending on your age
(e.g. Hart & Damon, 1986).

The concept of self has been described as *unique* (Fiske, Kitayama,
Markus, & Nisbett, 1998) and is an integral part of being human
(Lewis, 1990). At an early age understanding who we are is often
based upon simple things such as physical characteristics and
whether we are female or male (Montemayor & Eisen, 1977).
As people become older the idea of who they are becomes more
complicated. The focus is more on how people are thinking and
feeling and how others view them (Hart & Damon, 1986; Harter,
2003; Livesley & Bromley, 1973), even though gender and physical appearance still play a part. Psychologists have suggested that
individuals start forming their adult personality during adolescence
(Erikson, 1968) but that it can take long into adulthood before they
have established who they really are (e.g. Meilman, 1979).

The fact that people's identities become increasingly complex
with age means that there are many sources that directly or indirectly play a part in identity formation and maintenance, the
media being one of them (e.g. Brown, 1995; Wattanasuwan, 2005).
People's core values and beliefs often derive from the media (e.g.
Stutman, 1993), and continuous exposure to messages informing
us that owning the 'right' products can make us the 'right' sort of
person does inevitably affect identity and beliefs. Marketing messages help to establish what products and possessions mean (e.g.
Brown, 1995; Baudrillard, 1998) and it is the underlying meaning
that is the reason why possessions are part of people's identities
(Brown, 1995; Baudrillard, 1998; Elliott, 1997; Firat & Venkatesh,
1995).

## Using goods to underpin self-identity

It is not a modern phenomenon that consumption can construct
or reinforce people's identities. As early as 1890, James discussed
how people's extended self involved possessions and the experience attached to those possessions. But perhaps the extent to which
people are currently using possessions to express who they are is
the result of post-war mass manufacturing. During the 1950s and
1960s it was found that people see their possessions either as a
part of their identity or as an extension of themselves (Prelinger,
1959; Secord, 1968). This is particularly evident from a study

that specifically investigated the car product category (Pontiac and Volkswagen). It was found that there was perceived similarity between a car owner's self-image and the image of other owners of cars of the same brand. Additionally, it was also found that they viewed themselves as being different from those who owned a car from the competing brand (Grubb & Hupp, 1968).

— Ordinary products used in everyday life are directly or indirectly expressing who we are. Even simple things that may seem insignificant, such as what we eat for breakfast and whether we choose to read or to watch television in the evenings, are all self-expressive (Kleine, Kleine, & Kernan, 1993). Whether consumer activities are perceived to be more or less significant, they all contribute to our sense of identity (Belk, 1988; Holbrook, 1992; Kleine et al., 1993; Kernan & Sommers, 1967; Solomon, 1983).

It is evident from gender identity studies that expressing who we are through the use of products starts at an early age. Among those as young as two there are apparent sex differences in toy choice (e.g. Golombok & Hines, 2002; Maccoby, 1998, 2000). Boys tend to prefer transportation toys, blocks and other activities that involve gross motor activity. Girls on the other hand tend to show preferences for dolls and dressing up. The idea that certain toys are more or less closely linked to boys' or girls' identities is then continuously the reinforced in the form of the sex-role stereotypes that are commonly used in the mass media (Smith, Cowie, & Blades, 2003). This is the start of a process whereby people become socialised into using products and services to construct who they are (e.g. Benson, 2000; Dittmar, 1992; Elliott & Wattanasuwan, 1998). The outcome being that people's self-perception is often directly synonymous with the material possessions they have (e.g. Belk, 1988; Josselson, 1994) and their self-worth is linked to what type of products and services they buy (Kanner & Soule, 2003). Consequently, when consumers are trying to decide whether to buy something they ask themselves if it mirrors who they are (Dittmar & Beattie, 1998), as it is important that the products they buy represent who they are or who they wish to be.

It is difficult to determine when products are part of people's core self and when they are part of an extended self (Dittmar, 2008). Objects as self-extensions can include possessions such as books, houses, cars, clothes and jewellery (Belk, 1988, 2000). But equally the very same possessions may also at times be an integral part of self (Dittmar, 1992). Nevertheless, possessions to some extent contribute to sense of self, regardless of whether they are part of the core self or the extended self.

Because people's identities are often closely linked to their possessions, losing an item closely linked to self can lead to a loss of extended self (Dittmar, 2008). The loss of valuable objects has been linked to psychological distress (Benight et al., 1999). Something that becomes evident when earthquake victims reported that the favourite possessions they had lost were closely linked to their identity (Ikeuchi, Fujihara, & Dohi, 2000).

## Symbolic value of possessions

Consumers assign meaning to products and services (Gardner & Levy, 1955) and through this assignment of meaning brands can be used to enhance consumers' self-identities (Levy, 1959). Ultimately, it means that people are no longer purchasing products for their functionality but rather they buy them for their symbolic value (Elliott, 1997).

It has already been briefly mentioned that the underlying values of material possessions are often established and reinforced by the media (e.g. Brown, 1995; Baudrillard, 1998). They present people with ideas in regard to what the products that people use stand for (Jung & Lee, 2006). Equally, the people who are using them also shape the value of the products, and it does not have to be a 'real life' person; it can also be a fictional character (Cooper, Schembri, & Miller, 2010). For example, James Bond is a well-known character that has helped to shape the way in which we view many brands as being luxurious and exciting. When people are watching a *Bond* film they are inadvertently learning to attach social and contextual meaning to the brands and products featured in the film (Cooper et al., 2010), thus learning the symbolic value of different types of possessions.

The outcome of being continuously subjected to the signs and images which marketers make use of to 'seduce' consumers is that we make use of symbolic resources in order to help us make sense of everyday consumption (Wattanasuwan, 2005). In this way people are able to create the lifestyles that they desire by purchasing the products that are congruent with how they wish to live (Holbrook & Hirschman, 1982).

## ➤ Need for self-verification and enhancement of self-image

The symbolic value of possessions can be used for self-verification purposes. People commonly have a need for self-knowledge and this includes self-verification (Escalas & Bettman, 2003). In order to self-verify people tend to seek out life aspects that are consistent with their self-conceptions just as they tend to avoid those that are inconsistent. Consistency gives people the feeling that the world is predictable and controllable (Swann, 1990). Generally two types of different strategies are used to achieve self-verification: seeing more self-confirmatory evidence than actually exists, and attempting to influence other people's reactions by developing a self-confirmatory social environment (Escalas & Bettman, 2003). The latter of the two is more directly linked to consumption in that people can use possessions to display identity cues, perhaps by wearing a certain clothes brand or by driving a particular car (e.g. Schlenker, 1980; Swann, 1990). In this context consumers tend to choose products based on their need for self-consistency. Hence they select products by matching themselves to prototypical users (e.g. Niedenthal, Cantor, & Kihlstrom, 1985; Setterlund & Niedenthal, 1993). For example, a consumer who thinks of himself as an animal rights activist purchases the type of cosmetic products that he thinks other animal rights activists would purchase and use. Such consumer engagement may also be explained by the need for self-enhancement, as the person who sees himself as an animal rights activist also ensures that he becomes more like the desired prototypical user. Consequently, the consumer may reinforce his self-image (Escalas & Bettman, 2003).

### Judging others by their possessions

People use material possessions as a general guide to making inferential judgements about others. What people wear is commonly used to determine their personality (Gibbins & Schneider, 1980) and how to behave towards them (Bickman, 1971; Wise, 1974). Similarly, this also applies to a range of other products and services that we make use of, such as the magazines that people read (Munson & Spivey, 1980), the glasses people wear (Argyle & McHenry, 1971) and what cosmetics they use (Belk, 1978).

Such findings clearly demonstrate that material possessions can be utilised to communicate to others who we are. ⁓

## Group belonging

The fact that possessions can be used for communicative purposes means that they can be an important tool in bolstering social relationships (Elliott, 1997). Therefore consumption can be viewed as a cultural practice that is a way of participating in social life, whereby consumer goods are a form of social communication (Fiske, 1989). ⁓ Since the meanings of consumer goods stem from their social context (Douglas & Isherwood, 1979) it makes perfect sense that they can foster social relationships and group memberships. Hence consumer goods and services that a person uses can also help construct and maintain their group identity (Lunt & Livingstone, 1992).

## Effects of group memberships

Our social identities can define self in terms of the groups we belong to (Tajfel & Turner, 1979). Such a part of our selves can be very important to our self-concept. For example, it has been found that 46% of Americans felt that being an American (a social identity) was the most important thing in their life (Citrin, Wong, & Duff, 2001). At times when group memberships are an essential part of self, it will impact our overall behaviours and consequently it is possible that belonging to groups can be both positive and negative, depending on what types of groups we identify with.

One key reason why it is important to feel part of a group is because it has the capacity to increase self-esteem (Tajfel, 1981). This is because when you identify with a group, that group's prestige and status in society gets attached to your self-concept (e.g. Major, Sciacchitano, & Crocker, 1993; Tajfel, 1981). It also means that if they are associated with a group that is not perceived in a positive manner, people are less likely to mediate positive self-esteem (e.g. Crandall, 1994). Evaluations of oneself such as self-esteem can be used as an indicator of general well-being (Dittmar, 2008). However, it is not always as straightforward as saying that positive group memberships increase self-esteem, which in turn enhances well-being. For example, there are occasions when people may strive to belong to 'desirable' groups and the result is engagement in behaviours that are detrimental to psychological and physical health, such as compulsive buying or maladaptive eating patterns (Dittmar, 2008).

## Consumer behaviour as the result of group identity

On a behavioural level, commitment to groups is usually associated with pro-social behaviours in that individuals will behave in a way that is viewed positively by fellow group members (e.g. Ellemers, De Gilder, & Van den Heuvel, 1998; Simon, Stürmer, & Steffens, 2000). This can involve purchasing a product that is considered representative of what the group stands for. Thus, consumption patterns can be one activity that may be viewed as a way to conform to group norms (e.g. Doosje, Ellemers, & Spears, 1999; Terry & Hogg, 1996). The need to conform to group norms can also function as a direct or indirect pressure upon consumer-related activities, which is directly coupled to people's need to feel group belonging (Major et al., 1993). In such situations people can feel compelled to purchase products for the purpose of demonstrating group affiliations (Reingen, Foster, Brown, & Seidman, 1984; Wallendorf & Arnould, 1988). For example, clothing is one obvious way of signifying group membership (Solomon, 1985).

It is often during the early stages of group affiliation that many seek to buy products that can augment the feeling of belonging to the group. In particular, those who are high in self-monitoring (Bearden & Rose, 1990), or have a strong collectivist orientation (Cialdini, Wosinska, Barrett, Butner, & Gornik-Durose, 1999) are susceptible to what is deemed the group norm and wish to adjust to it.

The kind of groups that people wish to belong to may not always be of a small and concise nature. It may be that they wish to belong to a particular category of people, such as those deemed masculine or fashionable, and those groups in particular are often targeted by marketers.

## Marketing aimed at groups

Because advertising agencies are aware of people's desire to belong to specific categories of people, they often make use of this in marketing campaigns. Products are related to the aspirations and

emotions of their target audiences (Martineau, 1957) in an attempt
to capture their attention and interest. Advertisers often create a
'brand personality' that is preferred by certain categories of people. The result being that consumers tend to choose brands that are
congruent with who they want to be (e.g. Helgeson & Supphellen,
2004; Krohmer, Lucia, & Bettina, 2006). For example, people
generally have a clear perception of which brands and products
are gender appropriate (e.g. Allison, Golden, Mullet, & Coogan,
1979; Alreck, Settle, & Belch, 1982; McCracken, 1993). So when
an individual wishes to be viewed by others as being masculine
they simply buy products they think reinforce others' perception
of them as being masculine, which may include products such
as Marlboro clothes and cigarettes. Men in particular are often
reluctant to purchase something that can be viewed as feminine
(Jung & Lee, 2006) as it may tarnish their masculine image. For
anybody familiar with the Marlboro advertising campaigns featuring rough-looking cowboys, it is easy to see how stereotypical
images of brands are generated through well-thought-out marketing campaigns (Jung & Lee, 2006).

## When the users affect product categorisation

Product and brand categorisation does not have to be the result
of advertising. It can also be established through use by a particular group of people, such as lawyers or artists. Consequently
when people wish to demonstrate their social affiliations they can
make use of products such as clothes and accessories to show their
belonging (Solomon, 1985). Something that becomes even more
likely when people feel uncertain about their own capabilities of
becoming a member of a group. In such cases people use the symbolic value of material possessions to try to identify with the group
and to make the group believe that they fit in. This was found
in a study where a group of students on a business course who
lacked the ability to do well were much more likely to wear expensive watches and fancy business suits than those who were likely
to do well (Wicklund & Gollwitzer, 1982). By making use of the
products that would communicate to others that they fitted in,
the products helped to enhance their own identities as successful
business students. Similar results were also found in a later study
where law students were compared to already practising lawyers

(Wicklund & Braun, 1987). When both groups were asked how a lawyer can be identified, the students said by their personality and clothes, again demonstrating that material possessions are important when individuals are striving to become part of a particular group. By visibly showing that they belonged to the category of lawyers, it may be that the law students compensated for their own lack of ability (Wicklund, 1999). Both of the aforementioned studies show that individuals who aspire to be part of a particular — group of people will study what kind of material possessions the group uses in order to ensure that they make use of the same type of possessions. The studies also show that some products are more closely associated with certain types of groups.

## The downside of trying to establish an identity in a consumer society

The idea that 'by buying goods, we can magically acquire a different persona' (Dittmar, 1992, p.2) may be appealing to some. However, the process of making people change their identities through the use of material possessions has a less appealing side to it, the one where the main aim is to make money. Selling products is a money making business and in the hope of increasing sales figures advertisers may make use of techniques that can lead to feelings of discontent. Equally, exposing people to unrealistic ideals can also lead to feelings of dissatisfaction just as failure to 'purchase' an identity can.

## Making consumers feel discontent

Advertising's role in shaping the 'meaning' of possessions is perhaps inevitable as data suggest that people are exposed to somewhere in the region of 3,000 advertisements on a daily basis (Brower & Leon, 1999). Through use of slogans and clever imagery such messages tell consumers that they will not be complete without what is being advertised. Famous slogans such as 'The car in front is a Toyota', 'Maybe she's born with it. Maybe it's Maybelline' and 'Born to perform' (Jaguar) are all good examples of how adverts suggest that we are in some way inadequate but at the same time offer us a way to become more desirable. Slogans that are intended to play on people's insecurities make consumers feel dissatisfied (Richins, 1991) and it is the feeling of discontent that makes them buy products they may never otherwise have considered. As one advertising chief executive so aptly put it: 'It's our job to make women unhappy with what they have' (cited in Seager, 1993, p.120).

## Exposure to unrealistic role models

Social psychologists have established that people generally have a need to compare themselves to others (e.g. Festinger, 1954; Suls & Wheeler, 2000). The comparison process is very quick and happens automatically. At times people engage in what is called 'upward social comparison', which is when you compare yourself to others who are better than yourself in some way (Blanton, Buunk, Gibbons, & Kuyper, 1999). Humans do this to establish what they need to do to improve so that they can strive to become better; hence people will only engage in comparison when they feel it is relevant to them. When engaging in upward social comparison it is not uncommon that individuals compare themselves to people they are exposed to through the media. Bearing in mind — that the media contains a high number of unrealistic images, such as very thin models and pictures of people that have been severely airbrushed, it is highly likely that it will be very difficult, if not impossible, to achieve the goals a person sets themselves (Dittmar, 2008). Consequently such comparisons can make individuals feel depressed and think less of themselves (Wood, 1989). For example, when women who do not feel at ease with their figure read magazines containing pictures of skinny role models it can leave them feeling physically inferior (e.g. Groesz, Levine, & Murnen, 2002; Richins, 1991; Trampe, Stapel, & Siero, 2007).

Children in particular are sensitive to the frequent consumer messages that somehow propose what people ought to look like in order to be desired. For example, girls are exposed to unrealistic expectations of beauty by playing with dolls such as Barbie and Sindy, both of which have amazing figures that are impossible to achieve in real life (e.g. Dittmar, 2008; Moser, 1989). Additionally, the toys in question are also marketed as having lots of nice clothes and driving fantastic cars. Bearing in mind that children often internalise the consumer messages they come across, it is unfortunate that young girls view toys such as Barbie as role models (Pedersen & Markee, 1991; Turkel, 1998). Because children are exposed to such a high number of unrealistic images and they do not have the capacity to question them, they often become socialised into thinking that they are the norm (e.g. Frederickson & Roberts, 1997; Pope, Olivardia, Gruber, & Borowiecki, 1999; Wiseman, Gray, Mosimann, & Ahrens, 1992).

## What happens if consumers fail to purchase their desirable self?

When individuals realise that who they really are is not the same as who they wish to be, they can become very distressed (Higgins, 1987, 1989, 1999; Higgins, Klein, & Strauman, 1987). It may be that you wish to seem desirable to a group of people that you see every week at the local golf course. Because all the others at the golf course wear expensive clothes and jewellery you go off and buy several very expensive new outfits. Having bought the outfits you feel that you really belong to the group and you start to think of yourself as a person who is a popular member of the local golf club. As time goes by this feeling grows stronger. Unfortunately, a year later you happen to overhear a conversation where one of the club members you really like says that they think you look ridiculous in your outfits. The same person also goes on to say that the club really should not let people like you join as you are not what they deem to be a 'true' golfer. Hearing this you realise that who you are and who you aspired to be are not really the same thing and consequently you experience feelings of dejection, dissatisfaction and sadness (Higgins, 1989).

When individuals are faced with an inconsistency between who they are and who they wish to be, they may try to reduce the discrepancy by blaming others (Arkin & Maruyama, 1979; Davis & Stephan, 1980). For example, in the aforementioned golf club scenario the person who tried to make an effort by buying new clothes might say to themselves that the group they overheard was being unfair and that the group itself did not really fit in at the club. And who are they to criticise your dress sense when they really don't dress that well themselves? This shows that people do have some coping mechanisms in place in the event that they experience emotional turbulence as the result of having doubts about their self.

## Summary

Consumers are frequently purchasing goods and services in order to express who they are. This can be because society (through marketing and other users) has created symbolic meanings for products. Products are often purchased in the hope that they will make the purchaser feel as if they belong to a particular category of people. People have a need to feel that they belong to groups as this enhances their self-esteem and general well-being.

At times people try to use products to 'create' a self that they aspire to. However, such attempts can lead to feelings of dissatisfaction. One of the underlying reasons why it happens is because the self that people wish to be is often unrealistic and based upon unrealistic images that are portrayed in the media.

**To have is to be**

Gina is a 31-year-old mother of a girl aged 10 months. She lives with her husband in an affluent area of London. She is currently on maternity leave but intends to return to her work as a trainee lawyer when her daughter turns one.

Whilst Gina was pregnant she attended pregnancy yoga classes in the area where she lives. She used to discuss what kind of things she would buy for the baby with her classmates. When doing so she often found that all the other expecting mothers intended to purchase very expensive and 'fashionable' items that Gina could not afford on her salary as a trainee solicitor. Even though she never told anybody, she wished deep down that she too could afford to buy the same kind of things as the other mothers.

One item in particular that she was concerned about was the pram since it is an item that would be on constant public display. All the other expectant mothers said that they were going to buy a Bugaboo Cameleon, 3 in 1 travel system, which costs around £600. There was no chance that Gina could afford one. However, she tried to persuade herself that it did not matter and she ended up buying a good solid pram from Mothercare for only £250.

After the birth, when she started using the Mothercare pram, she noticed that the only other people in the area with a similar type of pram were those who lived on nearby council estates. This troubled her as she did not wish to be perceived as an uneducated individual with a low income, which is how she thought that others perceived the mothers living on council estates.

During her coffee mornings with other mothers from the yoga and NCT classes she had attended, she was on several occasions reminded of the fact that she had not bought a Bugaboo. It was continuously pointed out to her how great Bugaboo prams are. Because of this she felt as if she had picked an inferior pram and subsequently stopped using it. Instead she started using her Babybjörn carrier, which most of the other mothers she socialised with also had.

Gina has decided that if she has any more children once she has become a fully qualified lawyer and has a better salary, she will buy a Bugaboo pram so that the rest of the world can see what kind of person she really is.

## TO THINK ABOUT:

1. If people are what they have, then do they actually have a genuine identity?
2. Is there one true concept of self, or is it continuously changing – and the possessions we purchase with it?

## FURTHER READING THAT MAY BE OF INTEREST:

The following books should be of interest if you wish to find out more about the topics covered in this chapter:
- Dittmar, H. (Ed.) (2008). *Consumer culture, identity and well-being: The search for the 'good life' and the 'body perfect'.* Hove, UK: Psychology Press.
- Lane Benson, A. (2000). *I shop therefore I am: Compulsive buying & the search for self.* Northvale, NJ: Jason Aronson.

## FILMS:

Watch a *Bond* film (ideally one of the more recent ones). Before you do, write down the personality characteristics you think that James Bond has. Whilst you are watching the film, make a note of the products that are used in the film. Afterwards discuss what you think the products featured in the film represent. Are they in line with the personality characteristics you think Bond has? Perhaps they can be used to reinforce a particular archetypal myth of a lover or a hero?

## USEFUL WEBSITES:

To learn more about the topics discussed in this chapter you may wish to look at the following websites:

- **American Psychological Association:** http://www.apa.org/monitor/jun04/driving.aspx
- **British Psychological Society:** http://www.thepsychologist.org.uk/archive/archive_home.cfm/volumeID_17-editionID_105-ArticleID_684-getfile_getPDF/thepsychologist%5C0404ditt.pdf

# 3

# Consuming the Environment

What is the real cost of the goods and services that consumers are purchasing? Is it reflected in the price? Or is the price only part of the real cost? These are perfectly valid questions if one considers that consumers are not only consuming goods and services, but are also indirectly consuming the environment. There are currently 1 billion people on this planet that enjoy a high standard of material living. This is only a sixth of the population and many of those that do not currently have the same standard of living are striving to achieve it. If the planet's entire 6 billion population were to enjoy the same standard of living, another three planet Earths would be needed to support the level of consumption involved (Porritt, 2004). It is disconcerting that everyday consumer behaviours are continuously adding to the depletion of natural resources as well as harming wildlife worldwide, and the general consensus amongst many researchers is that 'runaway consumption' is a 'problem of growing proportions' (Amin & Thrift, 2005, p.230). One that is only set to get worse with the rapid growth of consumption in countries such as India and China (Stern, 2000).

## How consumption is contributing to environmental dilapidation

There are numerous different types of consumption that contribute to environmental decrepitude, and therefore too many to mention in one individual chapter. Consequently, what follows is an outline of a select few factors that are involved in causing environmental problems. The behaviours mentioned here are not in any way more or less important than those that are absent from the chapter. They are simply examples of environmentally destructive behaviour.

## Global warming matters

It is hardly news that global warming is something that many scientists are greatly concerned about (e.g. Oskamp, 2000; Taylor, 1999). The Earth's annual average surface temperature has risen by 0.51°C during the last 50 years. This is a clear sign of how global warming is rapidly spiralling out of control, as it previously took almost a hundred years for the same temperature increase to take place (Dunn, 2000). By the end of this century it has been estimated that the temperatures may rise even more, somewhere between 1.4 and 5.8°C (WWF, 2007).

Global warming is the cause of many serious problems. It causes our sea levels to rise, which leaves many people homeless (Flavin & Dunn, 1999). Moreover, global warming is damaging areas used to grow crops (Flavin & Dunn, 1999) as well as altering the global landscape (Stiglitz, 2008). Two parts of the world in particular clearly demonstrate geographical changes: the Aral Sea in central Asia, which has been reduced by 75% in the past 40 years, and Lake Chad, which has shrunk by 95% since 1963 (Taylor, 2007) (see Figure 3.1). Such changes are at the very least partially caused by global warming (e.g. Bomford, 2006; Gore, 2006; Parry, Canziani, & Palutikof, 2008; Taylor, 2007; Williamson, Saros, Vincent, & Smold, 2009).

In parallel with the temperature increase, the Earth will also suffer from an increase in hurricanes, flooding, and severe storms. The devastation that can be caused by such natural disasters was evident from the damage caused by Hurricane Katrina in New Orleans in 2005.

Reportedly Katrina took 1,800 lives and caused approximately $81 billion worth of damage (US Department of Health and Human Services, 2010).

Additionally, rising temperatures are also likely to reduce the profitability of farm land in India (Mudur, 1995; McSmith,

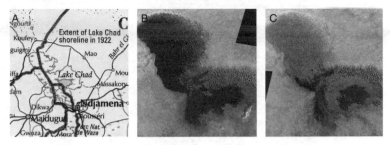

Figure 3.1　Impact of global climate change on Lake Chad

*Notes*: Figure A shows the outline of Lake Chad as it was in 1922. Photograph B was taken of Lake Chad in 1972 and photograph C was taken in 1987. From the three images it can be seen that the lake has greatly decreased in size.

*Source*: Figure A: Courtesy of www.timesatlas.com © Collins Bartholomew Ltd. Figures B and C: Images reproduced by kind permission of UNEP.

2006) and cost Bangladesh approximately half of the £58 billion (approximately $115 billion) that it has received in aid from other countries (McSmith, 2006). However, it would be naïve to say that such events are caused solely by consumers' everyday actions, but nonetheless they contribute, whether directly or indirectly, to the dilapidation of our environment (Stern, 2000).

There are many different types of consumer activities that contribute to global warming. Every time somebody drives a car or flies on an aeroplane they are contributing to pollution and consequently also to global warming. Transportation is one of the main contributors to carbon emissions and it is currently also the fastest growing one (Dow & Downing, 2007; Sheehan, 2001). In 2000, the transport sector emitted 36% more greenhouse gases than in 1990 (Geographical, 2008). The consumer lifestyle is said to be responsible for this increase, as it encourages people to purchase cars and motorbikes as well as increasing the mobility of goods and people (Dow & Downing, 2007; Geographical, 2008). In the US, the majority of households own at least one car and between 1984 and 2001 there was a yearly increase of 3.6% in mileage driven. Such an increase makes transportation the largest contributor to greenhouse gas emissions in the USA (Geographical, 2008). To get a clearer overview of how transport emissions are spread across the globe see Figure 3.2.

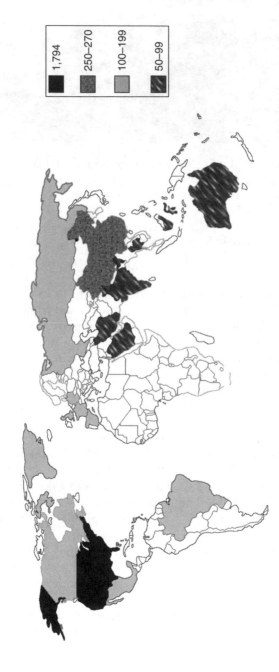

Figure 3.2   $CO_2$ emissions in 2003 (million tonnes)

*Notes*: The map shows the total carbon dioxide released from all domestic transportation in 2003. Data from countries/regions that are not filled in are either below 50 million tonnes or unknown.

*Source*: Adapted from Geographical (2008).

| | |
|---|---|
| ■ | 1,794 |
| ▨ | 250–270 |
| ▨ | 100–199 |
| ▨ | 50–99 |

In the next few decades this will only become worse as developing countries such as India and China will rapidly increase their transport usage. Estimates suggest that motorisation is likely to double between 1997 and 2020 (Sheehan, 2001), but it is possible that the actual figure will be a lot higher, depending on the speed of development in countries such as India and China. Additionally, it has also been projected that total passenger journeys by air (worldwide) will rise from 3.9 billion in 2004 to a staggering 16 billion in 2050 (Geographical, 2008; Bisignani, 2011).

Livestock animals also contribute to global warming as they account for around 10% of all the greenhouse gases released into the air (Gold, 2004), including nitrous oxide, carbon dioxide and methane emissions. In the UK it has been estimated that livestock enteric fermentation is responsible for as much as 95% of the methane produced from farming (Garcés, 2002). It is not only livestock farming that releases carbon dioxide into our environment, but indeed most food production that uses energy drawn from fossil fuels also releases carbon dioxide. However, there is a significant difference in the amount of carbon dioxide released into the atmosphere depending on the type of food produced. For example, to produce one calorie of protein from soya beans it takes two calories of fossil fuel compared to fifty-four calories to make one calorie of beef protein. Hence, a decrease in meat consumption would lead to a much needed reduction in carbon dioxide.

Global warming is also affecting sea life that is already severely damaged by overfishing and pollution. Fish and other aquatic species face many difficulties when the waters become warmer. For example, a high number of fish species cannot survive in water temperatures that are not within the range that nature intended them to be in. Furthermore, warm waters also make parasites that cause fish diseases to become more powerful (WWF, 2007). Overfishing of certain types of fish is certainly not helping and during the last two centuries there has been a rapid decrease in cod numbers in the Atlantic Ocean, leaving a rather uncertain future for the cod population (e.g. Mieszkowska, Sims, & Hawkins, 2007; Ottersen & Sundby, 1995). Let's not forget that sea life is not only a food source for humans; it also absorbs high levels of carbon dioxide. With the dwindling number of trees in the world to soak up carbon dioxide it is important to try to keep life in the ocean healthy and thriving.

## Deforestation

Fish are not the only animals that are affected by ruinous consumption practices. Cutting down the world's forests has a detrimental impact on animal wildlife too, as it endangers species that are already low in numbers such as gorillas and exotic birds (e.g. the *Francolinus nahani*). Consumption of paper products and timber is substantially contributing to the destruction of forests worldwide and the usage of such products does not appear to be slowing down. Every year 300 million tonnes of paper is produced (Wood Consumption, 2007). A large proportion of the paper goes into producing junk mail; yearly millions of households worldwide have hundreds of pieces put through their letter boxes (e.g. Abramovitz & Mattoon, 1999) and in the UK this is likely to increase in the next few years (Hickman, 2010). Most junk mail is randomly distributed to individuals who often have no interest in the products and services that are being promoted. Therefore it is hardly surprising that a large proportion of junk mail is put straight into the bin. In the US alone it has been estimated that around 10 billion mail-order catalogues are thrown out yearly (Abramovitz & Mattoon, 1999).

The festive Christmas season also contributes heavily to paper wastage. Approximately 1 billion Christmas cards are sent in the UK each year. For every 3,000 cards made one tree is chopped down (Recycling Consortium, 2007). The production of paper is also contributing to emissions of greenhouse gases (Hekkert, van den Reek, Worrell, & Turkenburg, 2002). At this point in time it does not appear as if there will be a reduction in paper consumption any time soon and estimates suggest that by 2015 a staggering 53 million tonnes of paper will be used for communication purposes (Hekkert et al., 2002).

Sadly it is only about 10% of all the paper consumed that is used for products that have longevity, such as photographs or books (Mattoon, 2000). This coupled with the fact that most of the paper products produced are not made from recycled paper (approximately 40%) (Ince, 1994) must make us question whether it is feasible to continue to consume paper-based products at the current rate.

Deforestation is bad news for many reasons but in particular because forests absorb harmful $CO_2$ emissions, prevent

destruction of wildlife and make natural disasters such as flooding and landslides less likely to happen (Abramovitz & Mattoon,
1999).

It is not always obvious how the products that consumers purchase contribute to the destruction of the planet's forests. Ingredients
such as palm oil also gradually help destroy forests. Palm oil is
the second most commonly consumed oil and it can be found in
biscuits, shampoo, cosmetics, chips, chocolate, crisps, detergents,
toothpaste as well as many other products (Friends of the Earth,
2004). Due to the fact that palm oil is a lucrative market, countries
such as Indonesia are clearing tropical rainforests to make way for
oil palm plantations. Currently the rainforest in Indonesia is disappearing at a rate of approximately 2 million hectares a year, whilst
the oil palm plantations are constantly increasing. If this continues
then the Indonesian island of Sumatra will soon be left with no
forest at all (Jepson, Jarvie, MacKinnon, & Monk, 2001). But it is
not only happening in Indonesia and oil palm plantations are not
always the problem.

Recent media reports show that other countries such as Uganda
have faced similar problems when sugar cane farmers have been
keen to take over vast areas of nature reserves (The London Paper,
2007; Reuters, 2007). Luckily some nature reserves are safe due to
fierce campaigning by conservationists (Wildlife Extra, 2007).

## Global starvation

Around 16,000 children die from hunger-related causes every day
(Black, Morris, & Bryce, 2003), and there are approximately 820
million people who are seriously undernourished in the developing
world (Food and Agriculture Organization of the United Nations,
2006). This is partially due to food shortages and the problem will
only get worse as the world's population continues to grow. The population is increasing at a rapid speed. From 1800 to 1930 the world's
population doubled to 2 billion, but it only took until 1975 to double
the population again to 4 billion. The population count reached 5.5
billion people in 1995 and in December 2007 there were over 6.6
billion people on our planet (US Census Bureau, 2007; Veitch &
Arkkelin, 1995).

One reason why some of the population is starving is because
of overconsumption of certain food products, such as meat. For

every calorie of meat that is produced ten calories of vegetation are required (Ehrlich & Ehrlich, 1990; Hardin, 1993). Livestock is fed on corn, grain and soya, which are all also suitable for human consumption. Hence if humans were to eat less meat there would be an increase in the amount of vegetarian food available for human consumption. It is therefore disheartening to hear that meat demand is expected to increase to around 327 million tonnes by 2020. That is over a 60% increase since 1997 (Gold, 2004). The more meat that is consumed, the more feed will have to be grown for the livestock to eat. If the meat consumption trend continues, the world's livestock will be consuming the same amount of resources as 4 billion people by 2050 (Tudge, 2004).

## Is it possible to reduce consumption?

Is it possible to encourage consumers to reduce their consumption? Can psychologists help make consumers become aware of the issues involved in non-sustainable consumption? Will such awareness become apparent in their consumption patterns?

Currently it appears as if environmentally friendly consumption is not always at the top of the list of priorities for consumers. However, there seems to be a growing concern for sustainable consumption and new creative ways of manufacturing are proof that it is not all doom and gloom (Michaelis, 2003). Even though a high proportion of people in Westernised countries are well educated and often realise that they are responsible for making environmentally correct consumption decisions, this awareness does not always translate into actual behaviour (Carrigan & Attalla, 2001; Vermeir & Verbeke, 2006).

At present there are few psychologists who are researching the impact of consumption on our environment. This is unfortunate as many believe that psychologists can make a vital contribution to changing people's consumption behaviours (e.g. Clayton & Brook, 2005; Du Nann Winter, 2003; Schmuck & Vlek, 2003), especially as psychology can strengthen the 'interdisciplinary science of human-environment interactions' (Stern, 2000, p.529).

By making use of a wide range of methods, it is already possible to demonstrate that consumption behaviours can indeed be changed (e.g. Du Nann Winter, 2003; Stern, 2000). In order to do so it is imperative to use techniques that have clearly been shown to work rather than relying on 'ideas' based on what appears to be 'plausible' (Gardner & Stern, 1996). By using established methods such as those arising from behavioural, cognitive and social psychological research there is a suitable platform to build further upon. Hence what follows is an outline of research that can get us one step closer to understanding how people can be encouraged to engage in pro-environmental consumer behaviour and in turn ameliorate environmental problems.

## Pro-environmental attitudes – do they change consumer behaviours?

A high number of environmentally concerned groups and individuals seem to be distributing information on the basis that it will change people's attitudes and in turn their behaviour. Researchers generally agree that the link between attitudes and relevant behaviours is often weak (e.g. Kollmus & Agyeman, 2002; Hines, Hungerford, & Tomera, 1986; Staats, 2003), meaning that at times the information circulated to consumers about environmental matters will have no impact on their behaviour. This can be noted in cultures that hold strong pro-environmental beliefs but that lack a track record of engagement in environmental protection (Gardner & Stern, 1996).

It may seem logical to assume that attitudes predict behaviours but doing so often means that situational factors that can play an important part in the decision-making process are ignored. Naturally, situational factors cannot be disregarded and those who dismiss them would ultimately fall prey to 'a version of the so-called fundamental attribution error' (Stern, 2000, p.525), which is when people attribute 'another's behaviour more to internal than to situational causes' (Hogg & Vaughan, 2005, p.93). In any given environment where consumers make a purchasing decision, there will be a string of elements determining whether to go for the environmentally friendly choice. Two for one offers, how much money consumers have and whether a friend is urging them to buy a particular product are all examples of situational factors that can play a part in why consumers buy what they do. Hence, when looking at consumer choices it is also necessary to take a close look at the environment itself as well as how social influence plays a role in our decision-making (Olli, Grendstad, & Wollebauk, 2001; Cialdini, Reno, & Kallgren, 1990). The fewer external elements there are to distract them or reinforce a particular behaviour, the more likely it is that attitudes will influence a person's behaviour (Gaugnano, Stern, & Dietz, 1995). However, there are very few environments where the consumer is not bombarded with different types of products and information. This is why it is better not to rely solely on the idea that people's attitudes will guide them to make the right choice, since all the distractions will shift their focus away from their own beliefs. Instead it may be better to look at situational and personal factors that are known to impact specific behaviours (Black, Stern, & Elworth, 1985; Stern, Dietz, Abel, Gaugnano, & Kalof, 1999).

## Strongly held attitudes

Even though the link between attitudes and relevant behaviours is often weak, one should not disregard the usefulness of consumers having pro-environmental attitudes, especially if the attitudes are strongly held. In such situations attitudes are often likely to guide their behaviour (e.g. Fazio & Zanna, 1978) as well as enable them to resist persuasion (e.g. Bassili, 1996; Krosnik & Abelson, 1992; Wu & Shaffer, 1987). The resistance to persuasion techniques is particularly important since we are frequently bombarded with messages to consume products and services that have a detrimental impact on our environment.

Strongly held attitudes are linked to our value systems in that values provide a structure that organises our attitudes (Hogg & Vaughan, 2005). Values can be good predictors of the choices people make (Verplanken & Holland, 2002) and certain types have been found to correlate with ecological behaviour (e.g. Dunlap & Van Liere, 1986; Lievers, Serra, & Watson, 1986). So if people consume in a pro-environmental way, 'they are expressing their value of respect towards nature by having a positive attitude towards buying ecological products' (Fraj & Martinez, 2006, p.134). Consequently, strongly held attitudes are important as they reflect the underlying values held by consumers.

Furthermore, attitudes are also important in that they can function as a good starting point when trying to get consumers to engage in environmentally friendly consumption. If people do not even hold pro-environmental beliefs, then it will be a lot harder to make use of other techniques in the hope of changing their minds. The bigger the discrepancy between personally held beliefs and a persuasive message, the less likely it is that the consumer will be persuaded (Petty & Cacioppo, 1986).

## How to create awareness

The first step in creating pro-environmental attitudes will be to ensure that consumers are aware of environmental problems and how they are affected by consumption. How the information is presented to them can be a determining factor. In particular there are three aspects that ought to be carefully considered when communicating environmental concerns:

1. Use strong visual images.
2. Keep it simple.
3. Don't ask for too much too soon (*take baby steps*).

### Visual imagery

Making use of words that can create strong visual images within consumers can play an important part in changing their attitudes and behaviours. This was demonstrated in the US when the following phrase was used to make people sign up for home energy audits: 'If you were to add up all the cracks around and under the doors of your home, you'd have the equivalent of a hole the size of a football in your living room wall.' Because people could clearly visualise what the problem was, a high number of people immediately signed up for home audits (Gonzales, Aronson, & Costanzo, 1988).

### Simplicity

It is not unusual for environmentally friendly messages (such as newspaper articles and anti-consumption campaigns) to contain jargon and scientific explanations. In order to fully understand them some previous knowledge of the area is required. Consumers often do not have the required knowledge to process the information that is available to them (Sanstad & Howarth, 1994). It is therefore important to present information in simple terms and in a way that fits in with what they already know (Costanzo, Archer, Aronson, & Pettigrew, 1986). Presenting information in a concise and specific manner informs consumers about exactly what they need to do, which then increases the likelihood of them engaging in environmentally friendly consumption.

## Baby steps

It is also important not to ask people to do too much too early on. This was found to be the case in a research study where signs were posted around a university building asking people to switch off the lights in unoccupied rooms. Such signs did not have an impact on behaviour and lights were still left on most of the time. It seems that asking people to continually switch lights on and off throughout the day was too much. However, when signs that asked people to turn out the lights after 5 pm were put up instead, the success rate increased by 60% (Cone & Hayes, 1980).

Similar steps also need to be taken when making use of advertising to create awareness of environmental issues. It has been found that advertising can be an effective tool in creating awareness and that this increases the likelihood of people engaging in pro-environmental behaviours at a later date (Kempton, Darley, & Stern, 1992), provided that it is properly structured. Additionally, it has also been established that adverts are more persuasive if they include an expert in the field (Hovland & Weiss, 1951; Jain & Posavac, 2001), preferably one who is attractive (Eagly & Chaiken, 1975; Petty, Wegener, & Fabrigar, 1997). Direct persuasion should be avoided as it can put consumers off; so also may a message that appears to be one-sided (Petty & Cacioppo, 1986). Hence, it is better to present a two-sided argument as long as the advertisement clearly and convincingly disproves the opposing argument (Allen, 1991; Crowley & Hoyer, 1994).

## Consuming purely for self-interest

One difficulty in regard to trying to change people's minds about their consumption behaviours is that if there is nothing in it for them personally then they are even less likely to consider it. This becomes particularly evident when a consumer is placed in a situation where they have to choose between purchasing something in their own self-interest and resisting for the 'common good'. The instant result of acting in the public interest is often not in the individual's own interest (Platt, 1973). For example, when you need to buy paper for your printer you know that it is much better for the environment to buy recycled paper, but as the recycled paper is more expensive you still buy the non-recycled kind as it will save you money. The consumer may be aware that buying paper contributes to deforestation and that it has a negative impact on our environment, but as they may not live to see the consequences of the world's forests disappearing they know it is not immediately applicable to them. The temptation to engage in non-environmentally friendly consumption is therefore much greater, as the rewards are immediate even if rather small. This is referred to as the 'Tragedy of the Commons' (Hardin, 1968, p.1243) and has been found to be applicable to environmental decision-making (Atran, Medin, & Ross, 2005). Luckily some researchers have established that it is possible to successfully implement specific strategies that will combat people's urge to act only out of self-interest (e.g. Berkes, Feeny, McCay, & Acheson, 1989; Deitz, Ostrom, & Stern, 2003).

Looking at behavioural research it can be noted that there are techniques that can be used to play on people's self-interest and consequently turn it into something useful. It is common knowledge that if a particular behaviour is positively reinforced it is much more likely to be repeated: giving people rebates, raffle tickets and cookies has been found to alter consumer behaviours (Everett, Hayward, & Meyers, 1974; Powers, Osborne, & Anderson, 1973; Walker, 1979). So by giving people an incentive (one that they value) it can be possible to change consumers' behaviours as it will be in their own interest. This may sound easy but we should not forget that any incentive given to people to engage in pro-environmental consumption must be more attractive than those promoting the use of products and services that are damaging for our environment. For example, the government may offer a tax rebate that will save every driver at least £300 a year if they choose to drive a car that is deemed better for the environment. This may seem to be a good incentive for car owners to trade in their old car. However, such an offer would be in direct competition to the kind of deals a car dealer can give you. Let's say that the environmentally friendly car costs £20,000 and that the driver is likely to use the car for a period of 10 years. The tax rebate would save the person £3,000 over that time period. Now let's imagine that a really attractive non-environmentally friendly car costs exactly the same and that the car dealer is prepared to give you £3,500 off the original price and throw in a free CD player. All of a sudden the non-environmentally friendly car may seem much more attractive.

## Comparing ourselves to others

The temptation to consume products that are not environmentally friendly, and that on many occasions consumers do not need, is also made worse by the fact that pro-environmental consumption is heavily influenced by people's social surroundings (Leonard-Barton, 1981). Consumers observe what others do and listen to other people's opinions. This is done so that we can compare our own actions to those of others to see whether we are acting in a socially acceptable way.

Bearing in mind that a high number of people indulge in over-consumption, most consumers think that it is acceptable to purchase numerous items, regardless of whether they are needed, as we socially compare ourselves (often subconsciously) to others (Festinger, 1954; Wills, 1981). Social comparison can make individuals feel better or worse about themselves depending on whom they compare themselves to (Marsh, Kong, & Hau, 2000). A common problem is that people often look at the material goods that others have and think that they may become happier if they have the same possessions. What stops them from buying even more products is their income, leaving many to think that if they could get a salary increase they would become a lot happier (Myers, 1993). However, earning more money and having more material possessions does not make people feel better about themselves (e.g. Myers, 1993; Kasser & Ryan, 1993, 2001; Sheldon & Kasser, 2001; Cohen & Cohen, 1996), but since consumers do not know this, their want for more continues to persist. Consequently they continue to compare themselves to those who drive a petrol guzzler or travel abroad four times a year, and subconsciously they believe that they will be happier if they can match their consumption behaviours and if finances allow, outdo them.

The way to gradually change this would be through creating an image of non-environmentally friendly consumption as being undesirable. If people whom consumers are comparing themselves to are against overconsumption, then it is highly likely that consumers will reduce their own consumption. In particular it may be a good idea to ensure that there are role models at hand when consumers encounter certain 'consumption situations' for the first time. This is because consumers are even more likely to engage in social comparison when there are no apparent standards to compare themselves against and when they feel uncertain about how to behave (Suls & Fletcher, 1983). The role models do not have to be anybody 'special' as people socially compare themselves to anybody present at the time they need behavioural guidance (Gilbert, Giesler, & Morris, 1995). For example, a lady called Sarah has just moved into a new neighbourhood when she receives a letter from the local authorities stating collection days for recycled rubbish. Since Sarah lives in a tiny flat with no real space to keep recycling boxes she is not very keen on recycling. However, as she wants to be liked by her new neighbours she decides to keep an eye out for whether her neighbours recycle. When Sarah realises that they do, she starts to recycle.

## Making people believe it is the norm to engage in environmentally friendly behaviour

The previous example of Sarah and recycling also demonstrates that people generally conform to what they perceive to be the norm. Norms are shared beliefs about how people should act (Schwartz & Howard, 1982), whilst social norms can be broadly defined as expectations of their behaviour held by social groups. Such expectations can be real or perceived but either way they make individuals adhere to social norms (Ajzen, 1988). Social psychological researchers have recognised for a long time the importance of social norms to fully understanding human behaviour (e.g. Berkowitz, 1972; McKirnan, 1980; Miller & Prentice, 1996; Triandis, 1977) and this knowledge has also been widely applied to consumer sciences.

Consumers conform to social norms by engaging in what are deemed socially acceptable consumption behaviours. These can be anything from buying a Gucci handbag (because all your friends have one) to avoiding sending Christmas cards (if your friends think that it is a waste of trees).

Because humans have a need to be liked and accepted by others, as this increases our self-esteem, it is not strange that consumers often conform to norms because they are worried that they may be poked fun at or excluded from a group. Something that is often notable in young children and the way they dress. Children tend to wear similar clothes to their friends' so that they will be liked and accepted by them (e.g. Creekmore, 1980; Rose, Shoham, Kahle, & Batra, 2006).

Though conforming to group norms in public is common, that is not to say that humans always privately agree (e.g. Levine, 1999; Nail, McDonald, & Levy, 2000). Their personally held beliefs may differ from those of the 'group majority', but nonetheless they will not act upon their own beliefs as they are worried what others may think.

Social norms can be used to change non-environmentally friendly behaviour. Support for this was found in studies investigating littering behaviour in public places (e.g. Cialdini et al., 1990; Krauss, Freedman, & Whitcup, 1978; Reiter & Samuel, 1980). The results showed that people were less likely to litter in places that were litter free and more likely to litter in an already littered environment. This is good news as it also brings hope that a number of other non-environmentally friendly consumption behaviours can be changed simply by making sure that people perceive avoidance to be the norm.

There is no doubt that one major hurdle to be overcome within the industrialised societies is that it is normal to overconsume. Everywhere we turn people are consuming products and services. Hence it is essential to change people's perception that consuming more than you need is the norm. This will not be an easy task and no doubt will take time. If psychologists could make consumers see that those who have high materialistic value orientations are not happier (e.g. Solberg, Diener, & Robinson, 2003) it would hopefully set us on the right course to save our planet.

## Summary

Consumption of goods and services can directly or indirectly contribute to the deterioration of our environment, such as global warming, flooding and deforestation. Typical examples of detrimental consumption activities include driving and the use of paper. Overconsumption in particular is a problem, which is why psychologists have proposed ways in which consumption can be reduced. Methods that can be applied include the use of persuasive messages, positive reinforcement and making people believe that it is the norm to engage in environmentally friendly consumption. The use of persuasive messages is aimed at changing people's attitudes and it is important to remember that a change in attitude does not necessarily lead to a change in behaviour. Even though the techniques mentioned can be useful they do not provide a 'magical' solution to how consumption can be reduced.

## Matsutake: a case of the Tragedy of the Commons

Every year as the summer recedes and rain begins to moisten the woods, thousands of people gather in the Cascade Mountain forests of Northern California and Oregon. They are all there for the very same reason, to collect Matsutake mushrooms (*Tricholoma magnivelare*). A lot of people have never heard of Matsutake mushrooms, but to Americans and Japanese they are very valuable and sought after.

The commercial harvest of American Matsutake mushrooms is a million dollar industry. The estimated size of the wild mushroom market (which includes Matsutake mushrooms) in the states of Washington, Oregon and Idaho in America grew from $21.5 million in 1985 to $41.1 million in 1992 (Alexander, Weigand, & Blatner, 2002). Prices per pound for the Matsutake range from $20 to $800 and they are often sold as delicacies to Japanese restaurants and stores. The profitability of picking mushrooms has led to an increase in the number of harvesters. No longer is it only people from the region who gather mushrooms; they also have stiff competition from migrant pickers who travel from outside the region and abroad. The camps that the gatherers set up can consist of as many as 2,000 or more mushroom collectors.

One problem is that many of the mushroom collectors do not know how to pluck the mushrooms properly. Inappropriate mushroom picking techniques affect the sustainability of the supply. If done well the root system remains intact and will continue to produce mushrooms year after year. However, if the collectors are inexperienced they are likely to damage the root system, gradually reducing subsequent fruiting. This is not only bad news because the mushroom will eventually disappear but also because the Matsutake is the fruit of a fibrous fungal body that spreads through the soil. Without the mushroom the forests in which they grow would be ecologically poorer places and parts of them may even die.

With a high number of individuals setting out to pluck the mushrooms, it is becoming fiercely competitive as each mushroom plucked converts into a decent amount of money. Consequently, the people picking the mushrooms are also less likely to show concern for 'good' picking practices as this would simply slow them down and potentially decrease a day's wages.

The mushroom pickers may be aware that the Matsutake are decreasing in number and that picking too many of them can damage the forest. However, as there are clear financial benefits to the individuals that pick the mushrooms, and the mushrooms are unlikely to disappear for good in the immediate future, most choose to continue to harvest the Matsutake.

## TO THINK ABOUT:

1. Do consumers care that they may be ruining our planet?
2. Who should ultimately be responsible for trying to save the environment, individuals or governments?

## FURTHER READING THAT MAY BE OF INTEREST:

If you wish to read more about psychology and environmental problems, the following texts might be of interest.

- Nickerson, R.S. (2003). *Psychology and environmental change.* Mahwah, NJ: Lawrence Erlbaum.
- Kasser, T., & Kanner, A.D. (Eds.) (2000). *Psychology and consumer culture: The struggle for a good life in a materialistic world.* Washington, DC: American Psychological Association. Chapter 5 discusses how psychologists can help save the planet.
- Du Nann Winter, D., & Koger, S.M. (Eds.) (2004). *The psychology of environmental problems.* Mahwah, NJ: Lawrence Erlbaum. Chapter 1 discusses how humans are gradually ruining the planet.

## FILMS:

There are few films tackling the topics covered in this chapter but it is definitely worth watching:
* *An inconvenient truth* (2006).

## USEFUL WEBSITES:

To learn more about environmental issues (and what you can do to help) you may find the following websites useful:
* **National Geographic:** http://environment.nationalgeographic.com/environment/
* **Nature:** http://www.nature.com/earthsciences/index.html
* **BBC:** http://www.bbc.co.uk/bloom/
* **Green TV:** http://www.green.tv/

# 4

# Ethical Consumption

If you had a choice as a consumer would you rather your favourite trainers were made by an adult earning at least a minimum wage or a young child aged 10 who gets paid around £4 per day? Would you rather that the pig whose bacon you ate in the morning had been well looked after or that it had been mistreated throughout its short life? I am guessing that most consumers would prefer if their shoes had been made by an adult who got paid a decent wage and that the pig that became bacon had been well looked after. However, unethical manufacturing practices are often 'hidden' from consumers so that they do not affect the consumer's decision-making process. Consequently, consumers are often unaware or uncertain of whether products represent an 'ethical choice'. Many organisations and individuals are campaigning for more transparency in manufacturing processes, which has resulted in the exposure of many familiar brands (e.g. The Times, 2007; Poulter, 2006). Such revelations are contributing to awareness amongst consumers which in turn will enable them to exercise the only power they have, their own individual purchasing power (Brenton & Hacken, 2006).

## Unethical manufacturing practices

Manufacturing practices that are considered unethical can be broadly defined as those that seriously damage the environment or a living being (Auger, Burke, Devinney, & Louviere, 2003; Michletti, 2003; Mintel, 1994; Shaw & Clarke, 1999; Shaw &

Shiu, 2003; Strong, 1996). Often they are divided into three categories (Lang & Hines, 1993):

1. *Human rights* (includes good working conditions and fair trade)
2. *Animal welfare*
3. *The environment*

The previous chapter looked at environmental issues of consumption and consequently this chapter will not revisit that area. Instead, it will focus on aspects linked to human rights and animal welfare issues.

## Human rights issues

The consumer market is full of cheap products and it is at times puzzling how prices can be kept so low. There are many possible explanations as to how prices are kept low and not all are linked to unethical practices. However, in some cases underlying explanations for overly competitive prices can be linked to exploitation of workers in less affluent countries. Well known companies such as Primark, Tesco, Matalan, Mothercare, Asda, Top Shop and Marks & Spencer[1] have all been accused by the media of unethical manufacturing practices (e.g. Daily Mail, 2007; The Times, 2007; Poulter, 2006). Claims have been made that Asian factories where adult workers get paid as little as 13 pence an hour are used by well-known clothes manufacturers (Daily Mail, 2007; The Times, 2007; Poulter, 2006) to keep Western prices down. Poor working conditions have also been found for children (see Figure 4.1). Child labour is not uncommon and currently there are over 200 million 'working children', of which 73 million are estimated to be aged under 10 (International Labour Organisation, 2007a). Every so often the Western media features shocking stories of child labour, and often they focus on the clothes industry. In recent years companies such as Gap, Nike, and Tesco have all been accused of using factories that employ children (BBC News, 2000; Islam, 2006; McDougall, 2007). And according to some reports, at times the children don't even get paid for their work as they have been tricked into working in factories (McDougall, 2007).

However, the clothes industry is not the only type of business that is using child labour. Children can be found working

Figure 4.1   Child at work

*Notes*: The picture was taken in Bolivia in 2010 on behalf of the International Labour Organisation, which is working towards the abolition of child labour. It shows a young girl carrying bricks in a brickyard in La Paz.

*Source*: Courtesy of International Labour Organisation © International Labour Organisation/M. Crozet.

on tobacco plantations in Mexico, where they are often exposed to large quantities of carbamic pesticides that are easy to inhale (Gamlin, Romo, & Hesketh, 2007). Unusually young workers can also be found in gold mines in Niger, as well as in bars and restaurants in Peru (International Labour Organisation, 2007b), to give a few examples.

The fact that children differ both physically and mentally from adults makes them particularly vulnerable in a working environment. Because children are immature they often fail to see occupational risks that are evident to adult workers and the result is that they are more likely to suffer from problems such as skin infection or injuries. Some young workers also endure long-term effects such as infertility, chronic back pain or cancer (World Health Organization, 2007).

## Animal welfare

Just like humans other types of animals are also subjected to serious mistreatment within the production industries. One aspect of manufacturing that has been heavily criticised is the way livestock is been treated. In particular, the debate has often focused upon the link between human health and what livestock animals consume. Animals that are bred to become meat produce are often fed large amounts of antibiotics in order to control staphylococci as well as to act as 'growth promoters'. Estimates suggest that approximately 11,000 tonnes of antibiotics are fed yearly to healthy animals in the US alone (Pretty, 2002). Such high consumption of antibiotics makes the animals and those who eat the animals gradually immune to them. Consequently, humans are a lot more vulnerable to illnesses as they can't always rely on antibiotics to cure them (Mellon, 2001). This is a problem that only seems likely to grow larger as industrial farming spreads across the world and many countries follow suit in the use of antibiotics (Robbins, 2001). The fear that this will have a detrimental impact on humans led the World Health Organization (1997) to call for a worldwide ban on the routine use of antibiotics as growth promoters, but no such ban has yet been implemented.

It is not only what animals are fed that is an ethical issue but also the way in which they are treated. Chickens are commonly housed in sheds containing 40,000 birds, with approximately 19 per square metre. The so-called broilers are fed high-energy cereal grains so that they reach a weight of approximately 2.5 kilograms in *less than 45 days*. Such rapid growth often leads to heart failure and puts immense pressure on their legs which often results in lameness. However, mistreatment of animals is not unique to chickens, as it can also be noted in the poor treatment of cows. The amount of milk produced has doubled in the last 50 years, partially due to high-energy feeding procedures that have been implemented for cows. Unfortunately lameness, milk fever and calving problems are some of the results of such feeding methods (Gold, 2004).

Animal welfare issues can also be seen in the manufacturing of cosmetics. One in three consumers around the world are spending more on beauty products than they used to (AC Nielsen, 2007) and in America it has been reported that approximately $8 billion is spent annually on cosmetics (Crossette, 1998). A high proportion of the beauty products used have been tested on animals. It is difficult to know exactly what goes on in cosmetic testing laboratories as the cosmetics companies are often not forthcoming with such information. However, it is known that Draize tests that measure levels of skin irritancy and eye tissue damage are commonly performed on animals (In Defense of Animals, 2007). During Draize tests, animals (most commonly rabbits) are kept conscious and restrained whilst they have substances dripped onto their eyes or shaved skin. They are then monitored for swelling and irritation of the eye or the skin. This can go on for hours or even days. The animals' eyes often swell and become highly irritated, and their skin becomes inflamed (Robinson et al., 2002). Most of us have at some point managed to get a small quantity of shampoo or soap into our eyes and it tends to be very uncomfortable. So it is easy to imagine how the rabbits must feel whilst having substances deliberately put onto their eyes.

The European Union passed a ban on the use of animals for testing beauty products which took effect in 2009 (European Commission, 2007), but as much testing on animals for cosmetic purposes takes place in America there is no real end in sight for animal testing. Perhaps the US can follow suit?

Thousands of animals are used for the testing of beauty products every year, despite there being no law stipulating that such products must be tested on animals prior to being released onto the market. It may seem relatively easy to implement a law abolishing animal use for cosmetic testing. However, at the time of writing there is no indication that the US will discontinue the use of animals for cosmetic testing purposes.

## Consumer awareness of ethical issues

It is difficult to know whether consumers are *aware* how products are made. There are those that argue that an increasing number of consumers do know how the products they buy are made (e.g. Barnett, Cloke, Clarke, & Malpass, 2006). However, market research sometimes indicates otherwise; for example, 48% of the American population are reportedly unaware that antibiotics are used in meat farming (Synovate, 2003, cited on FoodQuality News, 2003). Nevertheless, the fact that there has been an upsurge in sales of ethically manufactured goods and services (Szmigin, Carrigan, & O'Loughlin, 2007) seems to indicate some awareness, at least amongst a proportion of consumers. Even though some types of products (e.g. eggs) have seen an increase in ethical product choices to up to 40%, it is worth remembering that the overall market for ethically produced products is only around 2% (New Economics Foundation, 2005). Nevertheless it is clear that there are a number of ethically oriented consumers (Belk, Devinney, & Eckhardt, 2005), even though the discrepancy in estimates of their number may stem from the methods used to establish their existence at large.

## What is meant by an ethical consumer?

Ethical consumerism can be defined as addressing the social as well as environmental costs of global trade (Uusitalo & Oksanen, 2004). In order to be an ethical consumer, people can engage in two types of purchasing behaviour (De Pelsmacker, Driesen, & Rayp, 2005):

1. Buying ethically produced products (such as cosmetics that have not been tested on animals).
2. Boycotting products that have been non-ethically produced (e.g. not buying a rug that was made by a child).

Generally the literature on ethical consumers refers to the consumption of products but it is worth bearing in mind that it also includes services and various forms of practice, such as banking (Barnett, Cloke, Clarke, & Malpass, 2005).

## What happens when consumers find out about unethical practices?

The revelation that a company is engaging in unethical practices can have a more negative effect than the positive effect generated if a company is promoting good ethical practices (Folkes & Kamins, 1999). However, the revelation of unethical practices does not automatically mean that consumers stop purchasing the products and services concerned, because ethics are not usually considered in isolation from the product and brand (Crane, 2001).

Negative information about labour practices has been found to elicit emotional responses but not always enough to alter consumers' behaviours (Brenton & Hacken, 2006). This was found in a study where Oxfam's 'NikeWatch' campaign (an attempt to eradicate sweatshops) was used to investigate whether negative publicity alters consumers' attitudes and also their behaviours. Instead it appears that level of commitment to a company may guide the behavioural response produced to non-ethical practices (Ingram, Skinner, & Taylor, 2005). When consumers are highly committed they are prepared to forgive the company and continue to purchase its products, provided that the perceived harm is low. However, this can change if the level of perceived harm is high. In such instances consumers are less likely to be forgiving and consequently may boycott the products concerned (Ingram et al., 2005).

To what extent consumers are motivated to evaluate the negative information is also affected by their loyalty towards a company (Henard, 2002). Loyal consumers tend to focus on the relevance of the negative information and discount the actual negative information whilst simultaneously creating counter-arguments (Ahluwalia, Burnkrant, & Unnava, 2000). Hence, it is clearly more difficult to persuade those who are highly committed and loyal to a company that engages in unethical practices not to purchase its goods and services.

## Why do some consumers ignore information about unethical manufacturing?

Exposure to unethical practices through the media in the form of visual images can trigger strong emotional responses, which in turn may affect motivation to change (e.g. Sheppard, 2005). Very frightening messages can also lead people to feel helpless, and in turn think that what is happening is inevitable and that their own actions will not make a difference (Rosser, 1991). Some people find it difficult to deal with overwhelming emotional responses as they can lead to sadness, frustration, anger or anxiety. Because such feelings make consumers feel uneasy, they make use of coping responses (Lazarus, 1991). Coping responses can vary slightly in nature but the goal is ultimately the same, to reduce feelings of unpleasantness.

One easy way to reduce unpleasant feelings is to simply stop paying attention to the message that is upsetting them and consequently never find out exactly what unethical practices are taking place. The way around this is to present consumers with messages that induce 'moderate' fear as they are then more likely to process the information fully and be persuaded by the information presented (Devos-Comby & Salovey, 2002).

Consumers who don't ignore the information about unethically manufactured products and who happen to have a particular liking for the product concerned are likely to experience cognitive dissonance. This is when an unpleasant state of psychological tension is generated as the result of being aware of two pieces of information (cognitions) that are inconsistent (Festinger, 1957). Since people don't like to feel uneasy they naturally try to reduce the dissonance they experience, which may be done in one of the following ways:

- By looking for additional information to make one of the arguments stronger (e.g. the underpaid workers would not have a job and consequently no money at all if I did not buy this product),
- By changing one or more of the inconsistent cognitions (e.g. I will never purchase unethical products again) or
- By distancing oneself from the source of one of the cognitions (e.g. the paper that published the article suggesting a product was unethically manufactured tends to have a 'sensationalist' approach to journalism so the account is bound to be grossly exaggerated).

The language used to inform consumers about unethical manufacturing practices can also be a reason why consumers do not take the information onboard. Information presented to them is often complex and full of jargon, making it difficult for many to understand (e.g. Petty & Cacioppo, 1986). For example, when discussing how consumption affects the environment, terminology such as $CO_2$ emissions and burning of fossil fuels is commonly used. For those who have not previously heard about environmental problems in those terms, it can be difficult to process a message in which they are used. Consumers' ability to process the information fully and to elaborate upon what they have seen or heard depends on three factors in particular:

1. That they are motivated to think further about the message.
2. That they have previous knowledge of the area.
3. That they have enough time to think about what they have seen or heard without being interrupted (Petty & Cacioppo, 1986).

Due to the three aforementioned factors, it is important that the message itself clearly states the relevance to the consumer, so that they feel it is directly applicable to them and therefore feel motivated to listen to, read or watch the entire message. Keeping the wording simple and explaining any complex aspects in a clear and concise manner can ensure that no previous knowledge is required to deal with the message. However, the final factor presents more of a challenge. Consumers generally have very busy lives and it is almost impossible to present information of any kind to them at a time when they are unlikely to be interrupted by other messages, their children, their mobile phone, the radio or something equally common in today's society. But it may be possible to at least limit the number of interruptions by choosing to present a particular message at a time when children are likely to be asleep or when people are less likely to receive a frequent stream of phone calls, such as during early mornings or late evenings.

## Who consumes ethically?

Several attempts have been made to establish if certain people are more or less likely to engage in ethical consumption. From such research it is evident that it is not a simple process to try to categorise people into groups who are more or less likely to purchase ethical products and services. For example, Roberts (1996) found that clearly there are non-ethical consumers and that there is a weak relationship between social concerns and consumer actions. Others who have attempted to pinpoint differences based on characteristics such as age, gender, ethnicity, education and so on have found that it is difficult to use such information to identify 'responsible' consumers (e.g. Auger et al., 2003, 2004a, 2004b). Neither can country of origin be used as a determining factor, as Auger et al. (2004b) showed that people from the same country can rarely agree on the importance of different social issues such as labour and animal testing. In fact they found that there was more variance between individuals within a single country than between different countries.

## The link between thought and behaviour

It is evident from people's responses when they find out about unethical practices as well as the difficulty in pinpointing groups that are more likely to be ethical consumers that predicting or encouraging ethical consumption is not simple. Researchers continuously find that the issues consumers state that they care about do not necessarily correlate to their purchasing behaviour (e.g. Auger & Devinney, 2007). This has been echoed many times by researchers who have tried to understand the rise in awareness of ethical consumption issues and how they relate to actual purchase behaviours. Such attempts have often made use of the Theory of Planned Behaviour (Chatzidakis, Hibbert, & Smith, 2007), which proposes that purchasing intentions are determined by factors such as personal values, moral norms and internal ethics (Shaw & Shiu, 2002; Vermeir & Verbeke, 2007). In turn it has often been assumed that it's an individual's intentions that will directly determine a consumer's actual behaviour (e.g. Fukukawa, 2003; Ozcaglar-Toulouse, Shiu, & Shaw, 2006; Shaw & Shiu, 2002; Arvola et al., 2008; Vermeir & Verbeke, 2007). However, empirical evidence has clearly shown that ethical intentions rarely correlate with actual buying behaviour (e.g. Auger & Devinney, 2007; Belk et al., 2005; Carrigan & Attalla, 2001; Morwitz, Steckel, & Gupta, 2007; Young, DeSarbo, & Morwitz, 1998).

Rather than using consumers' intentions to try to predict ethical consumer behaviour it may be more fruitful to make use of measurements of past behaviour relating to social causes, such as being involved in an animal rights group (Belk et al., 2005).

## What makes consumers purchase ethical products?

Even though quite a lot has been written about ethical consumption, researchers do not really have a clear understanding of why some are more likely than others to become ethical consumers (Shaw, Grehan, Shiu, Hassan, & Thomson, 2005). Generally ethical issues are not high up on the agenda in terms of why consumers purchase products (e.g. Shaw, Shiu, & Clarke, 2000; Smith, 1987, 1990; Uusitalo & Oksanen, 2004); even sell-by dates have been found to be a more influential factor in the purchasing process (Harris International survey, 1995, cited in Oxfam Campaigns, 1996). That ethical issues are not necessarily a determining factor in regard to whether consumers will purchase products can be noted from real-life business examples such as Starbucks, which began offering Fairtrade coffee in its stores in 2001. Starbucks did this because of pressures from NGOs but has found that consumer demand is low (Argenti, 2004). So what factors do determine whether consumers buy ethically produced goods?

The nature of the product and the price seem to be key mediators between decision and purchase. For example, consumers concerned with price were less ethically oriented when faced with low-price, low-involvement products (such as soap). However, no relationship has been found between price sensitivity and ethical attribute sensitivity when consumers are faced with high-price, high-involvement products (such as sport shoes) (Auger et al., 2003, 2004a).

Whether products are made ethically or non-ethically also directly affects price. Elliott and Freeman (2001) found that products made under bad labour conditions are subject to high price elasticity whilst those made under good conditions tend to have low price elasticity. This seems to imply that companies will lose from having their products exposed as being manufactured under unethical conditions but have little to gain from ensuring that consumers know their products are ethically produced.

Cooper-Martin and Holbrook (1993) proposed that ethical consumption is 'affected by the consumer's ethical concerns' (p. 113). Such 'ethical concerns' are bound to be an integral part of the consumer's general belief system, which in turn will be based upon numerous values. Such values determine to what extent consumers want to take onboard information that they encounter about unethical manufacturing practices. The Value Theory (e.g. Rokeach, 1973) suggests that people's value orientations are general and relatively long lasting and that they guide how people think, feel and act. The more they value the information they have seen or heard, the more likely it will be to influence them to stop consuming unethically produced goods. Perhaps not surprising since values are a reflection of what is important to individuals. There is not an extensive amount of research that has been conducted in this particular area (e.g. Rawwas & Isakson, 2000), but it is generally accepted that values can be useful in explaining a wide range of consumption activities (Kahle, Beatty, & Homer, 1986; Rokeach, 1973; Schwartz, 1992). Examples of areas where values have been used to explain consumer behaviour include cigarette smoking (Grube, Weir, Getslaf, & Rokeach, 1984), organic food consumption (Grunert & Juhl, 1995) and Internet use (Schiffman, Sherman, & Long, 2003).

When attempting to identify what it is that causes consumers to become ethically oriented, researchers have looked at cultural personality types (Pitta, Fung, & Isberg, 1999; Rawwas, 2001; Singhapakdi, Rawwas, Marta, & Ahmed, 1999). Such research suggests that an individual's characteristics, shaped by their culture, will determine whether consumers want to buy ethically produced goods. Another area of research that has also been explored is the effect of collective behaviour upon ethical consumption (e.g. Chatzidakis, Hibbert, Mittusis, & Smith, 2004). Whether consumers value other people's opinion can be a determining factor in whether consumers engage in ethical consumption. The underlying values of the particular groups that consumers belong to will also be reflected in the individual's consumption behaviours. Meaning that consumers will try to adhere to the consumer behaviour that is approved by the group to which they belong (Chatzidakis et al.,

2004). Put simply, those who have a need to conform to socially desirable behaviour are more likely to avoid consuming unethical products than those who do not (Rallapalli, Vitell, Wiebe, & Barnes, 1994).

Perhaps the best way of understanding consumer engagement in ethical issues is to combine personal and social norms. For example, both types of norms have been found to play a significant part in the recycling decision-making process (Davies, Foxall, & Pallister, 2002). This indicates that engagement in ethical consumption is a complex process which is defined by the interaction between individual personality characteristics and in-group norms.

## Should consumers be held responsible for unethical manufacturing practices?

It is tempting to say that consumers should be held responsible for unethical manufacturing. If people stop consuming the products, the manufacturer will stop making them. However, a simple solution is not always the best one. Researchers have found that better ethical practices by business can affect ethical consumer behaviour. It may be that where businesses lead consumers will follow (Belk et al., 2005). However, this partially contradicts other findings previously discussed, that businesses do not stand to gain from promoting themselves as acting in a pro-social manner (e.g. Elliott & Freeman, 2001; Folkes & Kamins, 1999).

Companies may also be held responsible in terms of making it easier for consumers to identify ethically produced goods and services. Consumers often feel that they are unable to make an ethical choice due to the lack of information about how the items were made, especially when shopping for clothing items (Joergens, 2006). Hence it may be advisable for manufacturers to clearly label their products as being ethically produced.

Another reason why it is difficult to 'blame' consumers for unethical manufacturing practices is that clever marketing techniques are used to emphasise other aspects of the products that are not in any way linked to ethics. Techniques that make consumers forget about ethics include the use of celebrities in advertising and nice colourful packaging that distracts consumers' attention. This combined with the fact that it can be difficult to find out how products are manufactured should perhaps let consumers off the hook. Maybe instead it is the manufacturer's responsibility to ensure that goods are ethically produced? Or perhaps it is up to politicians to put laws in place that ensure that only ethical practices are used? Nevertheless it should not be forgotten that consumers can have a great impact on altering bad practices by boycotting unethically produced products (Brenton & Hacken, 2006).

## Summary

Products are not always manufactured using practices deemed ethical. It is difficult to say how aware consumers are of unethical practices but clearly the increase in sales of ethically produced goods suggests that at least there are some who know about the detrimental aspects of manufacturing. Consumers who are exposed to unethical practices do not automatically change their purchasing behaviour, especially if they are 'loyal' customers of the product or brand concerned. Many also ignore information about unethical practices as they find it upsetting. To try to prevent this from happening it is imperative that information is presented in a way that makes this less likely to happen. Unfortunately, consumers are often more concerned about sell-by dates and the price of a product than they are by whether it has been ethically produced.

### Listen to the consumer

In 2006 Marks & Spencer announced that it was converting all its coffee and tea to Fairtrade, as well as an additional 36 product lines including formal shirts and organic cotton baby wear. Since Marks & Spencer is an own-brand retailer it was at the time in a unique position to make the change. This was done as a direct response to consumer feedback. Stuart Rose, Marks & Spencer's chief executive, said, 'Our customers have told us they care about how our products are made and we want to help them make Fairtrade part of their retail habit' (Fletcher, 2006).

The switch towards Fairtrade products was ultimately the result of a survey that Marks & Spencer had previously commissioned. It showed that consumers are becoming increasingly 'ethically minded'. Of those that took part in the survey, a third reportedly had put clothes back on the rails because of concerns about how they had been produced. Similarly, this was also found for other products, since as many as one in five had left products on the shelves as a result of concerns about how they had been made. Seventy-eight per cent said that they would like to know how the products are manufactured. Also, 59% of the respondents said that they were already purchasing Fairtrade products and 18% said that they would if such items were more widely available.

Marks & Spencer's change seemed particularly timely as figures released by the Fairtrade Foundation also showed increased consumer demand for Fairtrade goods. The sales of ethical products grew by more than 50% during 2004. Also, the estimated value of UK retail sales of Fairtrade coffee alone was around £137 million in 2008, whilst the total amount for all Fairtrade products is in the region of £700 million (www.fairtrade.org.uk).

## TO THINK ABOUT:

1. Should consumers that purchase unethically produced goods be held responsible for how they are manufactured?
2. Are unethical manufacturing practices (e.g. human rights issues and animal testing) not unethical if the consumers don't mind?

# FURTHER READING THAT MAY BE OF INTEREST:

If you wish to read more about ethical consumption the following texts should be of interest:
- Harrison, R., Newholm, T., & Shaw, D. (2005). *The ethical consumer*. London: Sage.
- Nicholls, A., & Opal, C. (2005). *Fair trade: Market-driven ethical consumption*. Thousand Oaks, CA: Sage.

# FILMS:

If you wish to know more about America's food industry and how corporations often fail to consider what is best for all involved, take a look at:
- *Food Inc* (2008) (further information can be found at: http://www.foodincmovie.com/)

# USEFUL WEBSITES:

To learn more about ethical consumption the following websites should be useful:
- **Ethical consumer:** http://www.ethicalconsumer.org/
- **BBC's Religion & Ethics site:** http://www.bbc.co.uk/religion/galleries/consumerwaste/
- **Unicef:** http://www.unicef.org.uk/publications/pub_detail.asp?pub_id=5
- **Food Ethics Council:** http://www.foodethicscouncil.org/topic/Animal%2Bwelfare

## Note

1. Please note that the companies, such as Gap, Nike, and Tesco, included in this chapter have been accused *by the media* of engaging in unseemly practices. It is not the author's opinion that the companies in question have engaged in unethical practices. Readers are encouraged to make up their own minds in regard to whether there is any truth behind such accusations.

# 5

# Mirror, Mirror

Figure 5.1    Reflective beauty
*Source*:  Courtesy of Cathrine Jansson ©

> Mirror, mirror, on the wall, Who in this land is fairest of all?
> From *Snow White* (Jacob & Wilhelm Grimm, 1857)

That physical appearance is important is evident from research suggesting that the way people look is linked to well-being and happiness (e.g. Holder & Coldman, 2007; Neto, 2001; Stokes & Frederick-Recascino, 2003). People are often so concerned with physical appearance that it can affect the way in which others are perceived. For example, attractive people are often viewed as intelligent and sociable (Feingold, 1992), whilst those deemed to be unattractive, such as overweight people, are often seen in a negative light (e.g. O'Brien, Hunter, Halberstadt, & Anderson, 2007). It has been suggested that the consumer society is (at least partially) responsible for people's perceptions of others as well as for their fixations with physical appearance (e.g. Berry, 2008; Sarwer & Magee, 2006; Sarwer & Crerand, 2007). The consumer society is also said to encourage and discourage certain types of consumption linked to appearance such as cosmetic surgery (Sarwer & Magee, 2006; Sarwer & Crerand, 2007) and food consumption (e.g. Henderson, Coveney, Ward, & Taylor, 2009).

## A moment on the lips can be a lifetime on the hips

Clearly, food intake is indirectly a contributing factor in regard to whether people will be perceived to be attractive. In consumer societies slender figures are idealised, which may be one of the underlying reasons as to why obesity has been linked to a number of negative impacts, such as low self-esteem (e.g. Franklin, Denyer, Steinbeck, Caterson, & Hill, 2006) and emotional problems (e.g. Falkner et al., 2001).

People are increasingly becoming larger and a high percentage of the population are verging on being clinically obese. This is now such a serious problem that the World Health Organization (1998) declared obesity to be a global epidemic. Statistical figures on obesity are shocking: 25% of children and a staggering 61% of adults in the US are either obese or on the verge of becoming obese (National Center for Health Statistics, 1999; Troiano & Flegal, 1998). The statistical figures for the UK are also rather grim. In 2005, over 23% of the male population and over 24% of the female population were classified as being obese (NHS, 2006).

## Consequences of being obese

A string of research studies have found that obese children and adults are affected negatively by their weight. Obese individuals often suffer from different types of problems, including physical, financial and emotional difficulties (e.g. Dietz, 2004; Mellin, Neumark-Sztainer, Story, Ireland, & Resnick, 2002).

It has been found that overweight young children generally do less well at school (Datar, Sturm, & Magnabosco, 2004) and that overweight female teenagers often complete fewer years of school (Gortmaker, Must, Perrin, Sobol, & Dietz, 1993). Consequently, they are also less likely to go to college (Ball, Crawford, & Kenardy, 2004). Poor school performance may partially explain why obesity is more prevalent amongst women of lower socio-economic status (e.g. Moore, Stunkard, & Srole, 1962; Noppa & Bengtsson, 1980).

Obese people often fail to find loving companionships. Generally obese teenage girls and boys are less likely to date and have intimate relationships (Pearce, Boergers, & Prinstein, 2002), and obese adults are much less likely to get married (Gortmaker et al., 1993). The media may be partially to blame for people's failure to establish good loving relationships that provide solid social support. Since the media continuously emphasises that 'thin is beautiful' people are socialised to believe that obese individuals should not be objects of desire (Pearce et al., 2002). Therefore, it would seem that media socialisation is one underlying reason as to why overweight people fail to establish good social relationships. The lack of social support has also been linked to emotional instability in those that are obese and such volatility explains why they are more likely to have attempted suicide than slimmer individuals (Falkner et al., 2001).

Additionally, the emotional turbulence that obese people experience is likely to be further fuelled by the way in which they are perceived and treated by others. Research has found that obese individuals are perceived to be less intelligent, shy, and in desperate need of being liked by others (DeJong & Kleck, 1986). When people have a certain perception of others they often act in accordance with their beliefs and this will be reflected in the way they treat those that are obese. The misperception of what obese individuals are like is also likely to explain why obese individuals are often discriminated against in the job market (Wadden, Womble, Stunkard, & Anderson, 2002).

## Food advertising

The emotional turmoil obese people experience often further fuels their non-healthy eating and engagement in non-slimming activities such as watching television (Mellin et al., 2002). Whilst watching television they are frequently exposed to advertising that is encouraging them to consume unhealthy food products. Every year billions are spent on advertising foods that are heavy in fat content and research has found that there is a link between obesity and the amount of television that children watch (e.g. Crespo et al., 2001; Dennison et al., 2002; Dietz, 1996).

In the US young children see one food commercial every 5 minutes and of those approximately 90% are for high-fat foods and sweets (Horgen, Choate, & Brownell, 2001). Such figures are common worldwide, though some countries such as Australia (Morton, 1990), the UK and the US (Dibb & Harris, 1996) appear to show a higher number of food commercials. In most Westernised societies it has at some point been debated whether advertising aimed at children should be allowed, but little action has been taken against manufacturers wanting to advertise unhealthy foods to children. Children tend to be enticed by the high-fat foods and sweets shown on television, which will lead to such foods being preferred over healthier options (Horgen et al., 2001), which are rarely advertised.

## Availability of unhealthy foods

The fact that unhealthy foods and snacks are so easily accessible does not help either. Food outlets (especially unhealthy ones) are never far away. It used to be that people had to go to city centres if they wanted to visit a McDonald's or a Starbucks. That is no longer the case. Instead, fast food restaurants, coffee shops and minimarkets are everywhere, alongside the motorway, just outside old traditional villages, and in suburbia. With food becoming ever more accessible the number of obese individuals will also increase (Foreyt & Goodrick, 1995).

Consumers often buy food that is readily available. The further away consumers are from particular shops and restaurants (e.g. fast food chains), the less likely they are to use them (Ellaway & Macintyre, 2000). Hence if people happen to live in an area where the concentration of fast food outlets is high, then that will be what they eat (Reidpath, Burns, Garrard, Mahoney, & Townsend, 2002). Similarly, this has also been found for local supermarkets, in that the kind of food they sell will be directly linked to whether people consume nutritious food (e.g. Cheadle et al., 1991, 1995). This means that if supermarkets were to be more responsible in the choices of foods that they stock, it could have a positive outcome on people's bodyweights.

## The impact of price

Something else that can deter consumers from purchasing certain food products is price. Many shoppers do not wish to spend a large amount of money on food products and in particular on snacks. Consequently they often pick the cheapest option regardless of whether it is the most nutritious and the number of calories it contains (Glanz, Basil, Maibach, Goldberg, & Snyder, 1998). More often than not the cheapest options are the unhealthiest ones. This makes them particularly appealing for families with low incomes, where every penny often counts. Which will help to explain why many research studies have found that children and adults from lower economic classes are more likely to be overweight than those from higher economic classes (e.g. Miech et al., 2006).

There has been some success in increasing sales of healthy snacks when prices have been reduced. This has been noted when consumers buy snacks from vending machines. When the healthy snacks in vending machines are cheaper than or the same price as the unhealthy snacks, an increase in sales of healthy snacks has been the outcome (e.g. French, Jeffery, Story, Hannan, & Snyder, 1997). Perhaps if all healthy foods are subsidised so that overall lower prices can be maintained, we will also see a decrease in the number of overweight individuals (Wadden, Womble, et al., 2002). Rather than subsidise healthy foods and snacks, another alternative may be to tax the unhealthy ones (Jacobson & Brownell, 2000). Some say that it may be suitable to tax foods based upon the type and amount of fats they contain (Marshall, 2000). The question is how high the tax will need to be in order to act as a deterrent.

## Is the consumer society contributing to unhealthy eating habits?

No doubt there are consumer-related factors that play a role in whether people consume unhealthy foods. However, controlling for such factors does not necessarily mean that obesity will become a thing of the past as psychiatric disorders (Stunkard, 2002), parental influence (Birch, Johnson, & Fisher, 1995) and genetic predisposition (Chagnon, Perusse, Weisnagel, Rankinen, & Bouchard, 2000) may also play an important role in the current obesity epidemic.

Somewhere between 10% and 30% of all people who seek weight reduction have been found to suffer from a binge eating disorder (Spitzer et al., 1993; Stunkard, 2002). Binge eaters are set apart from people with other eating disorders in that they do not lose weight and they do not purge. The disorder is characterised by recurrent binges that individuals fail to control and feelings of distress about the bingeing episodes. Obese individuals that engage in binge eating are much more likely to have underlying psychiatric problems than obese individuals that do not binge eat (Wadden, Foster, Letizia, & Wilk, 1993; Specker, de Zwaan, Raymond, & Mitchell, 1994; Yanovski, Nelson, Dubbert, & Spitzer, 1993) and their condition is commonly coupled with depression, substance abuse, reduced social functioning, weight fluctuation and negative body image (Yanovski, 1993; Davison & Neale, 1998; Christenson et al., 1994). Hence, when binge eating is the result of a psychological condition, environmentally based changes cannot be the solution.

Children learn to like foods by being repeatedly exposed to them, meaning that they will learn to like foods through parental influence. For example, if a child is repeatedly encouraged by their parents to eat a snack they have not previously tried and at the same time sees that the parents themselves also eat and enjoy that particular snack, the child is more likely to also eat and enjoy that particular snack (Birch et al., 1995). Hence it is imperative that parents buy healthy foods to eat at home in order to encourage children to eat well at a young age. The problem is often that parents have very busy and stressful lifestyles, resulting in the use of ready-made meals that are often high in fat and sugars and not as nutritious as many other food options (Pusey, 2003). Consequently, children learn to eat the wrong kind of foods, a habit which is often carried through into adulthood.

In addition to psychiatric disorders and parental influences it is possible that genes play a role in whether people become obese. Even though no specific genes have been identified as contributing to obesity in humans a lot of research has been conducted looking at possible genetic influences (e.g. Campfield, Smith, Guisez, Devos, & Burn, 1995; Chagnon et al., 2000; Montague et al., 1997; Price, 2002). Genetic research has been promising but is unlikely to help combat the problem of a rapidly growing population of obese individuals (Wadden, Brownell, & Foster, 2002). Genes are likely to be a contributing factor but ultimately it is the environment that causes people to engage in overconsumption of unhealthy foods (Bray, 1998).

Overconsumption of food is a complex area. It is most likely an amalgamation of factors that, to different extents, contribute to the current problem of obesity. It would be a mistake to dismiss potential underlying causes, as food preference and consumption behaviour are multi-determined, meaning that factors such as advertising, accessibility of junk food outlets, socialisation, mental health and price of unhealthy foods seriously reinforce and aid consumption patterns that make people increase in weight (Story, Neumark-Sztainer, & French, 2002). One way to deal with the obesity epidemic might be to look at people's eating habits and what kind of activities they engage in (Hill & Peters, 1998; Price, 2002) and how they are reinforced by the environment (Wadden, Brownell et al., 2002). Whilst others suggest that public policy-making may be the way forward to ensure that obesity is not boosted by the environment (e.g. Horgen & Brownell, 1998; Nestle & Jacobson, 2000).

## Believing that less is more

It is not only foods with high fat content that are heavily advertised. So also are products and services that can help you achieve or maintain a skinny body frame. Whether we like it or not we live in a society that idealises slender women. The thin beauty ideal has pretty much been consistent since the 1960s (Wiseman et al., 1992).

A high percentage of women's body ideals are influenced by celebrities and fashion models alike (Garner, 1997). Women often compare their own figures with those of celebrities (Garner, 1997), which explains why they tend to feel worse about their own bodies after having read women's magazines and watched TV programmes that emphasise the thin beauty ideal (Fredrickson, Roberts, Noll, Quinn, & Twenge, 1998; Heinberg & Thompson, 1995; Levine & Smolak, 1992; Groesz et al., 2002). However, some are likely to be more susceptible to such messages than others (Thompson et al., 2002).

Body dissatisfaction is common in Westernised societies and children as young as 8 are reportedly unhappy with their physical appearance (Grogan, 1999). It has also been found that around about that age between 40% and 80% of young girls are already dieting (Stein, 1986) and that by the time they reach their early teens a large number of dieters are using purging, laxatives and diet pills to control their weight (Rodriguez, 1998).

## Eating disorders

In the industrialised world it is not uncommon for people to suffer from an eating disorder such as anorexia nervosa (e.g. Hsu, 1994; Walters & Kendler, 1994; Science Daily, 2007) or bulimia nervosa (e.g. Gotesdam & Agras, 1995).

Anorexia is a relatively common illness amongst women and in particular amongst young teenagers. It is difficult to say exactly how many women suffer from anorexia, but a recent study found that 2.2% of young Finnish women had a severe form of the illness and approximately 5% suffered from clear anorexic symptoms (Keski-Rahkonen et al., 2007). Such figures show that anorexia may be more common than previously thought.

Women of all ages diagnosed with anorexia are also frequently diagnosed with depression, panic disorder, alcoholism and obsessive-compulsive disorder (Kennedy & Garfinkel, 1992; Walters & Kendler, 1994). Additionally it has also been found that young adolescent women who endure a distorted view of their self and who believe that they need to be thinner are often also at increased risk of suicide (Overlan, 1996).

## The role of the media

The media's role in making women anorexic is frequently debated. Even though the media is likely to reinforce the thin ideal, it really needs to be remembered that it is impossible to hold the media wholly responsible for young women getting eating disorders. Eating disorders are psychological disorders and a single factor is unlikely to cause them (e.g. Walters, Neale, Eaves, Lindon, & Heath, 1992; Hsu, 1994) although a relationship between exposure to images of thin models and eating disorders has been found (Harrison, 2000).

Since anorexia typically begins in the early to middle teenage years, a time of insecurity and angst, it is very likely that media pressures may be what tip girls over the edge when they are already vulnerable. That vulnerable individuals are more likely to be affected by the media has been confirmed. In a longitudinal study it was found that only teenagers who already suffered from body dissatisfaction issues were affected by thin media ideals. However, other teenagers were not affected by increased exposure to pictures of thin models in fashion magazines (Stice, Spangler, & Agras, 2001). So even if the media may not adversely affect all people, it is likely to affect young consumers who are already in need of help and social support.

Since exposure to thin ideals makes vulnerable individuals more likely to commit suicide (Steiner-Adair & Purcell, 1996) and think less of themselves (Bessenoff, 2006; Stice et al., 2001; Groesz et al., 2002), should the media not make use of normal-sized models instead? The argument may be that thin models sell. However, sales figures have demonstrated that curvy figures can also increase sales and that people report a more positive body image after having been exposed to average or plus-size models (Groesz et al., 2002). One example of this is a series of ads and commercials used by Dove. Reportedly Dove attributed their 33% sales increase directly to ads featuring normal-sized women (Lee, 2005).

It is unlikely that advertisers will stop using thin women to promote their products and services. The use of those deemed physically attractive has been repeatedly found to capture consumers' attention and increase the likelihood of purchase (Halliwell & Dittmar, 2004). Thus it may be worth thinking about what can be done to prevent vulnerable young girls from falling into the body dissatisfaction trap. Continual interaction between adolescents and their parents is one way to deal with it. Teenagers who have parents that are involved in their television viewing have been found to have greater self-esteem and body satisfaction than those who don't (Schooler, Kim, & Sorsoli, 2000). Simply discussing what is seen on television may give children a more realistic picture of the world and hence in turn make them less likely to compare their own lives to what they see on the small screen.

Women are generally more dissatisfied with their appearance than men (Feingold & Mazzella, 1998). However, it has been found that men are also increasingly becoming concerned about their physical appearance (e.g. Harris & Carr, 2001; Demarest & Allen, 2000). That is not necessarily to say that men are experiencing the same level of dissatisfaction as women do. To date, little research has been conducted on how men are affected by thin male models portrayed in the media, but what findings there are seems to show that men do not feel as pressured to be slim as women do (e.g. Kalodner, 1997). Perhaps this is less due to socio-cultural pressures to be thin, as instead the media directly aimed at men seems to promote a well-built muscular body. Young men who read magazines containing overly muscular bodies have been found to be more conscious about how well-built they are and about beauty products for men (Hatoum & Belle, 2004). Hence, men are equally likely to be influenced by media images, but since the majority of the media images aimed at men do not contain thin models they are much less likely to feel that they need to take extreme measures to lose weight.

## Nip 'n' tuck

With the general trends and desires to look thin and beautiful there is constantly growing interest in cosmetic surgery and non-surgical treatments such as botox. In 2006 the British Association of Aesthetic Plastic Surgeons (BAAPS) (cited in Consulting Room, 2007) reported a 31% increase in cosmetic surgery in the UK. BAAPS members carried out 28,921 surgical procedures in 2006. Bearing in mind that not all plastic surgeons are BAAPS members the actual figures are likely to be a lot higher. According to

BAAPS, the most popular procedures are breast augmentation, eyelid surgery, liposuction and facelifts. Most non-surgical as well as surgical procedures were carried out on women but nonetheless over 2,000 men also went under the knife in 2006. It is not only the British population that is taking to self-improvements with the help of plastic surgeons, but indeed also all other Westernised nations. For example, in an Australian sample of 14,100 women, 7% reported that they had had some kind of cosmetic surgery done (Schofield, Hussain, & Loxton, 2002). That plastic surgery is becoming common can also be noted from statistics provided by the American Society for Aesthetic Plastic Surgery. It reported that over 11 million surgical and non-surgical procedures were performed in the US in 2005. That plastic surgery is becoming increasingly common in the US can be noted from phenomena such as giving breast implants as graduation gifts to female high school students (DeAngelis, 2005).

## Motivators to undergo cosmetic surgery

The research literature available has, to date, highlighted many factors in regard to why people are more inclined to have a favourable view of cosmetic surgery as well as why they would have it done (see Table 5.1). The different motivators appear to fall broadly into two categories: intrapersonal motives and social motives (Pruzinsky & Edgerton, 1990). Intrapersonal motives that have been identified include factors that are clearly focused on wanting to feel better about oneself. For example, those who experience body image dissatisfaction (e.g. Brown, Furnham, Glanville, & Swami, 2007), and those who link self-esteem to appearance (e.g. Delinsky, 2005), are more likely to hold pro-cosmetic surgery attitudes.

Social motives are those that focus on factors whereby cosmetic surgery becomes important due to friends and family. Examples of this include being teased by others if you do not look a particular way (Sarwer, Magee et al., 2003), observing those that are close to you (e.g. Swami, Chamorro-Premuzic et al., 2008), and internalisation of media messages (e.g. Sperry, Thompson, Sarwer, & Cash, 2009) that are based on the ideals portrayed in the media (Sarwer, Wadden, Pertschuk, & Whitaker, 1998). All are factors that have been found to predict interest in cosmetic surgery.

Mirror, Mirror 81

Table 5.1 Factors that affect whether people undergo cosmetic surgery

| Author/s | Year of publication | Identified reason |
|---|---|---|
| Sarwer et al. | 1998 | Body image dissatisfaction |
| Davis & Vernon | 2002 | Attachment anxiety |
| Sarwer, LaRossa et al. | 2003 | Basing self-esteem on appearance |
| Sarwer, Magee et al. | 2003 | Appearance related teasing |
| Delinsky | 2005 | If appearance is a contingency of their self-worth |
| Henderson-King & Henderson-King | 2005 | Fear of becoming unattractive |
| Sarwer et al. | 2005 | Internalisation of socio-cultural messages from media and entertainment industries |
| Brown et al. | 2007 | Body image dissatisfaction |
| Brown et al. | 2007 | Vicarious experiences of cosmetic surgery via family and friends |
| Henderson-King & Henderson-King | 2008 | Cosmetic surgery is positively correlated with attitudes about use of makeup |
| Swami, Arteche et al. | 2008 | Having previous experience of cosmetic surgery |
| Swami, Chamorro Premuzic et al. | 2008 | Vicarious experiences of cosmetic surgery via family and friends |
| Sperry et al. | 2009 | Internalisation of socio-cultural messages from media and entertainment industries |

Note: The content is organised by the year of publication.

## Links between cosmetic surgery and materialism

The fact that cosmetic procedures are generally not for people who really *need* to alter their appearance has led some to brand it 'retail medicine' (Fleming, cited in New South Wales Health Care Complaints Commission, 1999, p.170). Materialistic individuals and those who internalise socio-cultural messages have been found to be more likely to be accepting of cosmetic surgery procedures (Henderson-King & Brooks, 2009), reinforcing the idea that it is yet another consumable. People who are highly materialistic (see Chapter 6 for further information about materialists) are often less satisfied with their lives (Richins & Dawson, 1992) and tend to suffer from low self-esteem (Kasser, Ryan, Couchman, & Sheldon, 2003). Material are often motivated to engage in activities that are aimed towards life aspects that they aspire to, such as appealing physical appearance and high social status (Kasser & Ryan, 1996; Kasser, 2002). However, the satisfaction of achieving material goals tends to be transient and the outcome is that they will be dissatisfied once the novelty and excitement of a purchase have worn off (Kasser, 2002). The feelings of discontent will spark the search for another purchase that they believe will make them happy. Such patterns then continue in the form of a cyclical process whereby the materialist is on a continuous search for happiness through consumption (Kasser, 2002). It is in the light of this that Henderson-King and Brooks (2009) explain why materialists are more accepting of cosmetic surgery, as well as why some are more likely to undergo serial surgery in the hope of improving their physical appearance.

## Objet d'art or calamity?

Socio-cultural messages emphasise that 'it is important to be beautiful' (e.g. Bartky, 2003; Calogero, Boroughs, & Thompson, 2007). Those who fail to be perceived as attractive are often teased, stigmatised and discriminated against (Calogero, Herbozo, & Thompson, 2009; Crandall, 1994; Jones & Crawford, 2006; Puhl & Brownell, 2001), and consequently can be very sensitive to rejection based on their physical appearance (Park, DiRaddo, & Calogero, 2009). For those who do not think that they are attractive, the constant bombardment of messages reinforcing the idea that 'beautiful is good' makes them vulnerable to persuasive marketing messages, encouraging them to improve the way they look. Different consumer opportunities offer women chances to maximise their beauty potential and this is often done by making them feel inadequate and in constant need of improvement (Henderson-King & Brooks, 2009). The feelings of need to continuously improve make them more accepting of cosmetic surgery (Henderson-King & Henderson-King, 2008) and the outcome is that 'the female body becomes not only an object, but also a *project*, an object to be worked upon' (Henderson-King & Brooks, 2009, p.134).

Many research studies in different areas have found that individuals who are perceived to be attractive are often given preferential treatment and many more positive attributes by others than those who are not. For example, attractive individuals have been found to be less likely to be convicted for minor criminal offences and are perceived to be social, dominant and intelligent (e.g. Feingold, 1992; McKelvie, 1993). Hence it is easy to see why people want to improve their physical appearance. However, what if surgical treatment does not have the wished-for effect and leaves a person less physically desirable than before? Because of the possibility that cosmetic surgery can go wrong, it has been questioned whether those who do not really need plastic surgery ought to be targeted through marketing campaigns (Wolf, 1990). Negative outcomes of surgery may include facial immobility or bad scarring (Pridmore & Turnier-Shea, 2001).

It is also worth noting that researchers have found that even when surgery is a success, psychological complications may emerge in post-operative patients in the form of anxiety, disappointment and depression (Borah, Rankin, & Wey, 1999).

## Not just for women

Many assume that it is mainly women who are pressurised to look a certain way but the increase in men's consumption of cosmetic goods and services appears to be telling a rather different story (Wood, 1989; Macken, 1993; Bagnall, 1996). Men are not under the same kind of pressures as women are and consequently the kinds of cosmetic products and services that they consume are different. Nonetheless, both sexes often seem to take action due to pressures instilled by the media. A good example of how the media can instil physical insecurities can be noted in men's beliefs about penis size. As many as 45% of the male population are reportedly unhappy with their penis size (Lever, Frederick, & Peplau, 2006) and a common concern seems to be that they worry that their partner is not sexually satisfied (van Driel, Weijmar Schultz, van De Wiel, & Mensink, 1998). Such concerns are generally considered to be influenced by messages in the media that size matters as it is a sign of masculinity (Kilmartin, 2000; Lehman, 1993). Recent adverts for men's underwear for Armani and Calvin Klein have made use of footballers such as David Beckham and Freddie Ljungberg posing provocatively in tight pants that make them appear to be well endowed. Such images are sending out a message that successful and good-looking men do not have small penises.

Pornographic pictures and films also reinforce the same message that size matters. Men with small penises are unlikely to be featured as sex gods in pornographic movies. Instead pornography frequently features men with large penises and in most instances they are seen to be sexually satisfying women who use exaggerated responses in order to make sure that the viewer believes that penis size matters. Being bombarded with messages about penis size often makes men feel pressurised and such pressure can in turn make men feel very insecure and may explain why men are increasingly seeking out treatments such as silicone injections to make their penis larger (Templer, 2002).

## Money matters

The monetary cost of cosmetic procedures adds another dimension to the debate on cosmetic surgery. Partially the increase in cosmetic surgery in the Western world can be explained by larger disposable incomes (Thorpe, Ahmed, & Steer, 2004). However, cosmetic procedures are not undergone only by those who are relatively well off. Previously it was the case that only those who were better off would pay to become beautiful (Gare, 1999). However, this is rapidly changing as it is becoming increasingly common for those who can't afford to have cosmetic surgery to finance it by taking a loan. For example, in the US loan companies are offering their customers monthly payment plans for cosmetic procedures undertaken (Figueroa et al., 2000). It has also been reported that in Lebanon banks are providing loans for those who wish to improve their physical appearance with a few nips 'n' tucks. Apparently, in Lebanon consumers can borrow as much as £2,500 to improve their mirror image (BBC News, 2007). This is concerning as it encourages people to get into debt in order to have a procedure done. In Australia a survey found that around 23% of those who underwent cosmetic surgery had financed it by taking a loan or by putting it on their credit card (Committee of Inquiry into Cosmetic Surgery, 1999). So not only may consumers having cosmetic procedures done suffer psychological costs; they may be further burdened by monetary debt.

## Cosmetic surgery, friend or foe?

So far a number of less desirable aspects linked to consumption of cosmetic surgery have been pointed out. However, it is important to acknowledge that numerous studies have also found that those who have plastic surgery can indeed feel better about their overall body image and report an overall better quality of life. In a study conducted by Sarwer et al. (2005), it was found that as many as 87% of patients reported satisfaction with their post-operative outcomes. This included overall physical body image improvement as well as satisfaction with the appearance of the feature altered by surgery. Similar results have also been produced by a number of different studies (e.g. Cash, Duel, & Perkins, 2002; Young, Nemecek, & Nemecek, 1994) demonstrating that cosmetic surgery can be beneficial. There are those who suggest that some of the results produced in regard to post-operative outcomes are perhaps not as reliable as they ought to be due to the lack of valid and reliable instruments that have the capacity to accurately measure what they are intended to measure (e.g. Kosowski et al., 2009). Nonetheless it is likely that post-operative outcomes will be positive for at least some patients.

It has already been mentioned that psychological complications can be one negative outcome of having cosmetic surgery (Borah et al., 1999). However, such outcomes may be due to patients having unrealistic expectations so that they are unlikely to feel happy and content afterwards (Honigman, Phillips, & Castle, 2004). It is also possible that the reportedly high number that suffer psychological complications after surgery (Borah et al., 1999) can be explained by the possibility that they may have had a psychological condition prior to the operation, such as depression or anxiety (e.g. Honigman et al., 2004). Whatever the underlying reasons are for possible discontent post-operatively, it increases the likelihood that a person will have more procedures done (Honigman et al., 2004).

## Summary

The consumer society that we currently live in is undoubtedly pressurising people into believing that they need to look a certain way. Such pressure is turning individuals into objectified selves, meaning that people are constantly aware of their physical appearance. Consumption of fatty foods is contributing to many people feeling insecure and inadequate in their own bodies. It is possible to reduce the amount of junk food people eat by changing factors such as marketing, price and availability. Those who buy into the media philosophy that 'thin is beautiful' may find that they experience high levels of body dissatisfaction, so much so that they engage in maladaptive eating patterns. The media may also partially be responsible for people feeling that they need to undergo cosmetic surgery in order to be accepted by society as being attractive. Research suggests that alterations of physical appearance through surgery can lead to both positive and negative outcomes.

---

### Television, the creator of a thin ideal?

One famous study conducted by Becker, Burwell, Gilman, Herzog and Hamburg (2002) has clearly shown how Western television shows can influence the body preferences that people have. Bearing in mind that typical American shows have a high number of slim and attractive individuals in them, it is important to know whether such individuals have an impact on how the viewers think they should look.

Prior to 1995 the population of the Nadroga province of Fiji did not have television. However, that same year it was set to be introduced. This provided a team of researchers (Becker et al., 2002) with an ideal opportunity to investigate the effects of television upon young adolescent girls.

Before the arrival of television people had preferred fuller figures, which reflected the importance placed on insatiable eating. It was simply part of the culture that 'big is beautiful'. Big men had traditionally been seen as wealthy and powerful and big women as beautiful (Reynold, 1999, cited in Safir, Flaisher-Kellner, & Rosenmann, 2005). However, this was set to change when television was introduced into most homes almost overnight in 1995.

In 1995 before the advent of television, only 3% of Fijian adolescent girls reported ever vomiting to control their weight. By 1998, that number had increased to 18%. This is a 600% increase in bulimic behaviour in only 3 years after the introduction of television. The very same year 74% of girls also reported feeling 'too fat' at least sometimes and as many as 62% reported dieting during the past month.

Girls who watched television at least three nights per week were 50% more likely to perceive themselves as fat or overweight and 30% more likely to diet, even though the more frequent watchers were not more overweight.

## TO THINK ABOUT:

1. Should 'ideal' people be used in advertising? Or would it be better to use 'real' people?
2. Cosmetic surgery, is it a friend or foe?

## FURTHER READING THAT MAY BE OF INTEREST:

The following books should be of interest if you wish to find out more about the topics covered in this chapter:
- Berry, B. (2008). *The power of looks: Social stratification of physical appearance*. Aldershot, UK: Ashgate.
- Sarwer, D.B., Pruzinsky, T., Cash, T.F., Goldwyn, R.M., & Persing, J.A. (Eds.) (2005). *Psychological aspects of plastic surgery: Clinical, empirical, and ethical perspectives*. Philadelphia, PA: Lippincott Williams & Wilkins.
- Blackburn, G.L., & Kanders, B.S. (Eds.) (1994). *Obesity: Pathophysiology, psychology and treatment*. Boston, MA: Jones and Bartlett.

## FILMS:

You may wish to watch the film by Darryl Roberts about whether Americans are obsessed with beauty. It provides an insight into issues such as child models, plastic surgery, celebrity worship, and airbrushed advertising.
- *America the beautiful* (2007).

# USEFUL WEBSITES:

To learn more about the topics looked at in this chapter you may wish to look at the following websites:
- **World Health Organization:** http://www.who.int/topics/obesity/en/
- **Healthy Place:** http://www.healthyplace.com/eating-disorders/main/ eating-disorders-body-image-and-advertising/menu-id-58/
- **Food Standards Agency:** http://www.food.gov.uk/news/ newsarchive/ 2007/mar/tvads

# 6

# Consumption as a Means to Happiness?

These days, people are consuming far more products and services than they can possibly need. Bearing in mind that people are continuously subjected to a stream of marketing messages that suggests that 'owning a product equals happiness' (Kasser, 2002), it is not difficult to see why consumers are inspired to consume products and services they may not necessarily need. The question is, does consumption make people happier and overall more satisfied?

Since the 1980s there has been a lot of debate amongst researchers in regard to how overconsumption affects people. The general consensus is that consumption is not synonymous with happiness (e.g. Ahuvia, 2002; Kashdan & Breen, 2007; Roberts, Tanner, & Manolis, 2005). However, not everybody agrees and there are those that suggest that the right kind of consumption can have a positive impact on consumers (e.g. Van Boven, 2005). Belk (1985) suggested that it is essential to try to determine if materialism is a positive or a negative trait. Even though many have tried, it appears that there is no simple answer in regard to whether materialism is a friend or foe to humans.

## Materialists

It is becoming increasingly common that people have high materialistic value orientations (MVOs), meaning that they are frequently preoccupied with acquisition of material possessions and attaining financial success in order to purchase products and services (Kasser et al., 2003). Those who display strong MVOs often have a desire to compensate for a lack of self-worth, as well as lacking abilities to deal with general life challenges (Kasser et al., 2003). Additionally, a negative relationship has been found between materialism and subjective well-being, quality of life and overall satisfaction (Kasser, 2002; Richins & Dawson, 1992), which suggests that materialists are generally unhappy compared with those that are not materialistic.

## Becoming materialistic

Researchers have tried to pinpoint if there are underlying factors that can predict whether people become materialistic. To date it is still not entirely clear what exactly determines to what extent people become attached to material possessions, but there are some findings that suggest that when individuals lack something in their lives they are more likely to become materialistic. This is particularly evident from research investigating childhood issues. For example, it has been found that children whose parents are divorced are more likely to become materialistic young adults (Rindfleisch, Burroughs, & Denton, 1997). Such findings are not surprising as experiments suggest that insecurity produces materialistic tendencies (e.g. Chang & Arkin, 2002; Kasser & Sheldon, 2002; Kasser, 2002). It is likely that children are turning to consumption hoping to reduce stress caused by the family disruption (Roberts, Tanner et al., 2005). However, consumption does not appear to be a good coping mechanism as adolescents who associate happiness with material possessions have been found to experience higher levels of family stress due to parental divorce compared to those who do not associate happiness with material possessions (Roberts, Tanner et al., 2005).

Other factors that may affect MVOs include having been subjected to cold and controlling care by a mother during the teenage years (Kasser, Ryan, Zax, & Sameroff, 1995), and being subjected to socio-economic disadvantages (Cohen & Cohen, 1996; Kasser et al., 1995). It may be that childhood factors such as the aforementioned contribute to the likelihood that consumers later in life try to acquire material possessions that can gain other people's approval (Kasser et al., 1995).

Even though people's childhood may play a role in whether people become materialistic, that is not to say that it is the only underlying factor. When measuring MVOs it has been found that people sometimes consume in an attempt to alleviate their insecurities (e.g. Chang & Arkin, 2002; Kasser, 2002) and to conform to their social surroundings (Achenreiner, 1997; Schroeder & Dugal, 1995). This is the reason why high materialists tend to choose products that others will perceive to be expensive and high status (Holt, 1995; Richins, 1994; Wong, 1997), as it helps them to gain others' approval and to be viewed as enviable.

Furthermore, it has also been identified that those who are generally unhappy or uncertain about the meaning of their existence often become materialistic (e.g. Chang & Arkin, 2002; Diener & Biswas-Diener, 2002). When this is the case, consumers are often looking for 'a quick fix' to their problems. This may be in the form of purchasing a product that they believe will increase their appeal to others (Kasser et al., 1995). Such consumption is often encouraged by advertisers in that they make those with insecurities think that their lives will become better if they have the products advertised (Velasquez-Manoff, 2008).

The media in general may also be contributing to why people have high MVOs. From the moment people are born they are bombarded with media messages encouraging them to consume, something that has a bearing on their behaviour and thought processes (Kasser, 2002). People internalise the messages they are exposed to so that they become the norm. This happens because humans have a basic need to adopt cultural and familial values (Ryan & Connell, 1989), which are increasingly shaped by the media (e.g. Postman, 1985; Jackson Harris, 2004). Continuous exposure to television programmes such as *Deal or No Deal, The Price Is Right, Big Brother* and *Who Wants to Be a Millionaire,* where the aim is to win money and valuable prizes, sends viewers the message that being materialistic is not a bad thing.

The fact that the media often focus on the rich and famous also contributes towards materialistic behaviours as it has been established that it is common for people to model their own behaviour upon others they have observed (e.g. Bandura, 1977). Children are particularly likely to learn to be materialistic from their social surroundings, whether it is through observing their parents (Kasser et al., 1995), peers or heroes (Ahuvia & Wong, 1998, cited in Kasser et al., 2003). Hence, learning through the media can be primary or secondary: primary learning takes place when a child observes how a person behaves through newspapers, advertising and so on; secondary learning occurs when parents and peers engage in behaviours that they have copied from what they have observed through the media, which are then in turn imitated by the child. For example, materialism may be learnt through the media in the following way: a young girl's role model happens to be Victoria Beckham. The girl may read in the papers that Victoria Beckham changes outfits three times a day and that she is constantly following the latest fashion and that this is what makes her admirable. Therefore, the girl will wish she could have a lot of clothes so that she would also be seen in a favourable light by others. The fact that materialism is often coupled with a reward (i.e. admiration by others) increases the likelihood of people replicating the behaviour (e.g. Bandura, 1977; Skinner, 1953).

## Social implications of being a materialist

Having materialistic value orientations shapes the way in which people view life in general (Goldberg, Gorn, Peracchio, & Bamossy, 2003). In particular, it is clear that personal attributes assigned to others can be based on the material possessions a person has. This is supported by a study conducted by Dittmar and Pepper (1994), who found that UK-based adolescents perceived affluent people as being more intelligent, hardworking and successful. Interestingly enough the very same individuals were also rated as being less warm. Such perceptions appear likely to be cross-cultural as similar results were also found in a study conducted in the US. Skafte (1989) found that in a young American sample (aged 11–16) wealthy strangers were perceived in a more favourable manner than those who were less affluent. Participants were asked to rate a stranger on 20 personality-based traits. Strangers described as wealthy were seen as more intelligent, likely to get better grades and to make friends more easily. The fact that material possessions and wealth shape the way in which people are perceived tells us a lot about the society in which we live (Goldberg et al., 2003). It is likely that the higher the MVO, the more influential material possessions are in guiding people's values and beliefs (e.g. Dittmar, 2008).

## Materialism = unhappiness?

It is not easy to determine whether being materialistic increases or decreases people's general well-being and happiness. One factor that might cast some light on this matter is people's mental well-being.

Depression rates are generally higher in more economically developed countries (Buss, 2000) and the use of anti-depressants in Westernised societies has seen a steady increase since mass manufacturing started. This may suggest that there is a relationship between consumption and general well-being and happiness. However, it is not mass manufacturing per se that is causing people to feel depressed. Instead it has been proposed that the recurrent theme in marketing messages that happiness can be purchased (Kasser, 2002) may be responsible for the link between high MVOs and depression (Csikszentmihalyi, 2003). The media may also be responsible in that it triggers people to perceive themselves as failures as it continuously makes use of material possessions to emphasise people's success. This was proposed by Nesse and Williams (1994, p.220), who stated that

> Mass communications, especially television and movies, effectively make us all one competitive group even as they destroy our more intimate social networks. ... In the ancestral environment you would have a good chance at being the best at something. Even if you were not the best, your group would likely value your skills. Now we all compete with those who are the best in the world. Watching successful people on television arouses envy. Envy probably was useful to motivate our ancestors to strive for what others could not obtain. Now few of us can achieve the goals envy sets for us, and none of us can attain the fantasy lives we see on television.

Different psychological perspectives offer different solutions in regard to whether having high MVOs is good or bad. Sometimes the same psychological approach can even present different viewpoints. For example, the evolutionary approach appears to offer a two-fold solution as to why people consume. One aspect is that evolutionary theorists (e.g. Wright, 2000) have proposed that a desire to attain products and services can stem from the hope of making oneself more desirable as a mate or leader (Zahavi, 1975) by signalling one's status, resourcefulness and wealth through the possessions one owns. Such ideas indicate that consumption may be something positive in that it fulfils a practical function in society and will therefore encourage people to consume. However, others don't necessarily agree with this notion as they claim that overconsumption goes against the idea of 'Darwinian Happiness' (Grinde, 2005). Instead people should only consume items that are essential.

Even though there are some distinct theoretical differences most researchers in the area do not support the idea that consumption is something constructive (e.g. that it can be used to attract a partner, as proposed by some evolutionary psychologists). Socially oriented psychologists have managed to find emerging patterns in regard to what it is that encourages people to consume generally. Unfortunately, most of those patterns are linked to less positive factors.

## Social psychological view

Generally, research findings suggest that those with high MVOs are less satisfied with their lives (e.g. Richins & Dawson, 1992). This may be partially due to the fact that materialists tend to think that success is measured by how many and what kinds of possessions people have (Richins & Dawson, 1992; Holt, 1995). Those beliefs are in turn likely to be the result of too much television viewing (Sirgy et al., 1998), where accomplishments are more often than not symbolised by a flash car and a big house. When they see this, materialists base their real-life goals and targets upon those portrayed on television (Kasser, 2002; Braun & Wicklund, 1989).

Social psychologists have also proposed that the link between MVOs and low life satisfaction may be down to social support (Solberg et al., 2003). Evidently, materialists generally have fewer valued friendships. However, even if they managed to maintain high-quality relationships their overall life satisfaction might not be affected (Solberg et al., 2003).

## Humanistic approach

Making use of what the humanistic school proposed in terms of what motivates individuals, it can easily be understood why materialists are less satisfied. Both Maslow (1954) and Rogers (1963) believed that humans need to strive for self-actualisation in order to become complete as individuals. Self-actualisation involves an individual fulfilling their own potential and Maslow (1943, p.377) said that 'A musician must make music, an artist must paint, a poet must write, if he is to be ultimately happy. What a man can be, he must be.' However, prior to attempting to become self-actualised people have to fulfil a number of physiological and psychological needs. Meeting such physiological and psychological needs ensures that individuals have the basic essentials that are important for contentedness, such as food, shelter, safety, security, love and self-esteem. Only once these needs have been satisfied can a person focus their attention on becoming a complete individual who feels truly alive and knows how to perfect their life craft. Additionally, self-actualised individuals are also autonomous, unique and playful in their outlook on life.

Consumer behaviourists often misguidedly suggest that self-actualisation can be experienced by purchasing the right product or experience, perhaps by buying a Porsche or going bungee jumping. However, what Maslow was referring to is not something that could be fulfilled by one action but is something that would complete the individual as a whole for the remainder of their life. Consequently, it would not be possible to achieve self-actualisation by engaging in one kind of consumption activity. Neither would it be possible to fulfil all the other needs through consumption; for example, you can't buy love.

Because people focus so much on consumption activities when they become materialistic, they simply fail to strive for self-actualisation in an achievable manner. Rather than focusing on how to be creative and genuinely experiencing something life altering, they hope to fulfil their potential by purchasing a product or service in the expectation that it will alter their lives (Fromm, 1976). The fact that people focus so much on acquiring material possessions means that they are distracted from noticing intrinsic rewards (Deci & Ryan, 1985a) that can help them achieve self-actualisation. Such individuals have been found to have a personality tainted by how they let external sources guide their behaviours and beliefs (Deci & Ryan, 1985b, 1987). Not surprising then that those who have such personalities are less likely to self-actualise and are generally concerned about what others think (Deci & Ryan, 1985a; Koestner, Bernieri, & Zuckerman, 1992).

Putting it bluntly, materialists' constant pursuit of possessions makes them miss out on the true life experiences that are ultimately the path to happiness and self-satisfaction.

## Other possible explanations

Just because there is a negative relationship between consumption and mental well-being, it does not necessarily mean that it is consumption that is the cause of the negative state of mind. It is equally possible that individuals who are not in a good state of mind are seeking out consumer-related activities in the hope that they might make them feel better. There is certainly evidence to suggest that this is a possibility. For example, Chang and Arkin (2002) conducted three studies to test if people tend to engage in materialistic-oriented activities in the face of general life uncertainties. The results showed that individuals with self-doubt and those who felt that society lacks norms were much more likely to turn to materialism. So when people are feeling insecure about themselves and society, they are therefore also more likely to let other activities suffer as a consequence of becoming materialistic.

## Can consumption make people happy?

The negative impact of consumption discussed throughout the chapter certainly seems to indicate that consumption cannot make people feel happier on the whole. Researchers have found that individuals who are concerned with possessions and image generally feel less good about themselves (Kasser, 2002; Kasser & Ryan, 1993, 1996, 2001). The negative correlation between MVOs and well-being appears to be a worldwide phenomenon as samples from England (Chan & Joseph, 2000), Australia (Saunders & Munro, 2000), Germany (Schmuck, Kasser, & Ryan, 2000) and South Korea (Kim, Kasser, & Lee, 2003) all confirm that such a relationship exists. But perhaps it is not that people consume products and services that make them unhappy? Maybe it depends on what they are actually consuming and how often?

## Experiential purchases

Consumers that have been found to have high MVOs tend to value possessions that are expensive, are seen as high status and can easily be spotted by other people (Holt, 1995; Richins, 1994; Wong, 1997), whilst individuals who have been found to be less materialistic or not materialistic at all generally value experiences rather than possessions. Overall the latter have also been found to have greater life satisfaction and this is likely to be because they think experiences are more important (Holt, 1995; Richins, 1994). Previous research has found that strong and meaningful relationships and spiritual experiences make people feel generally better about themselves (Emmons, Cheung, & Tehrani, 1998; Kasser & Ryan, 1993; Myers, 2000). This has also been supported by Kasser and Sheldon (2002), who found that those who spend more time with their families and engage in religious activities during the festive Christmas period report higher levels of personal well-being, whilst engaging in the buying and receiving of gifts during Christmas leads to lower levels of well-being. So, what if people bought 'experiences' for their friends and family rather than just gifts? For example, it may be that giving your family a week away as a Christmas present will give you the perfect opportunity to spend some quality time together and in turn increase their well-being.

That experiences can make people happier than possessions was confirmed by Van Boven and Gilovich (2003) when they asked 97 undergraduates to rate how happy their most recent material or experiential purchase over $100 made them. Similar results were found in a follow-up study where 1,279 US citizens of varying ages reported that experiential purchases made them happier. In the latter sample group, it was also found that those with the lowest levels of income were just as likely to report that material possessions made them happy as that experiential purchases did. Van Boven and Gilovich explain this by stating that such findings make perfect sense as poorer individuals will normally have to try to fulfil their basic needs and have few resources that can be used for non-essential purchases. Hence, when buying something as a treat they may very well value it more than those who can afford to spend their money on experiential as well as material purchases. So perhaps if individuals who can afford to buy a lot of goods were more selective in their purchase choices, they might not feel so dissatisfied with what they had bought.

One reason why experiences are more valued than material possessions may be because they only exist as memories, as opposed to a product that will physically continue to be present once bought. It is common that people later forget the details of an experience that they found annoying at the time. Consequently, the memories can be altered to create a rose-tinted perspective on what actually happened (Mitchell, Thompson, Peterson, & Cronk, 1997), meaning that the consumer is left with a memory of a perfect experience.

Additionally, it has also been proposed that experiences help construct who people are and can therefore offer a greater hedonic value (Van Boven & Gilovich, 2003). For example, travelling through Africa with a backpack can make an individual feel adventurous and free-spirited and in turn they think of themselves as a daring person who likes a bit of excitement. Experiences are also something that people often find easier to discuss with others and consequently they also help to foster social relationships. As previously discussed successful social relationships have been found to make people feel happier overall (e.g. Diener & Seligman, 2002).

## Hedonism: a way to increase happiness?

It has been proposed that hedonism is a way of life (Veenhoven, 2003). When people are hedonistically oriented, they are open to pleasurable experiences. Ultimately, this suggests that for some pleasure seeking is the driving factor of human behaviour (Veenhoven, 2003). Seeking out pleasurable experiences may increase the likelihood of people coping more effectively with various problems in life. This is due to the fact that enjoyment generally raises people's tolerance levels for stress (e.g. Iverson & Erwin, 1997). Furthermore, when people enjoy themselves they generally become more sociable. For example, people talk and laugh more during an enjoyable dinner (Veenhoven, 2003). Such social activities may in turn also strengthen social relationships, which can in turn also contribute to feelings of overall happiness (Diener & Seligman, 2002). The positive side of hedonism supports Van Boven and Gilovich's (2003) theory that experiential consumption in particular may be good for consumers. But in theory it may also take the idea that consumption can be a positive thing one step further in that a pleasurable experience may involve other types of consumption, such as purchasing and using a new handbag or a television.

However, there are mixed opinions in regard to whether hedonism is good or bad. There has been a real debate trying to establish if it is a healthy life approach or simply a life of overindulgence and even moral decay (Veenhoven, 2003). One reason in particular as to why hedonists may end up unhappy is that pleasure can fade with time. 'This would leave the pleasure seeker unsatisfied and give rise to an urge for ever-stronger stimuli' (Veenhoven, 2003, p.439). Such an idea has been explored in what is known as the 'Hedonic Treadmill Theory' (Brickman & Campbell, 1971). This theory proposes that all people are stuck on a hedonic treadmill and that both good and bad events temporarily affect happiness, but that people quickly adjust and bounce back to hedonic neutrality. What this ultimately means is that any efforts made to increase overall happiness cannot succeed (Diener, Lucas, & Napa Scollon, 2009). This model nicely translates into hedonic consumer behaviour in that the more material possessions people have, the more material possessions they want. People's expectations of which material possessions are going to make them happy are constantly rising. Once they have a particular possession, they become accustomed to having it and it will therefore no longer make them happy.

## Summary

Can consumption make you happy? Overwhelmingly, research suggests that there is a negative relationship between consumption and general well-being. People who consume a high number of products seem to do so due to trying to fill a void in their life. In particular, feelings of insecurity have been linked to becoming highly materialistic and this in turn has also been linked to a need for approval. Those with high materialistic value orientations are likely to suffer since they strive for something intangible. Their constant pursuit of material possessions also makes them disregard aspects of life that can contribute to general well-being, such as friendship. At times, people with highly materialistic value orientations suffer serious psychological consequences. However, it is not possible to say for certain that it is their materialistic value orientations that are causing the problem. Instead it has been proposed that it may be *what* people consume that is the cause of their feeling more or less happy.

## Friends versus products

Carl is 42 years old. He lives in a big three-bedroom flat all by himself in the centre of Manchester. He has a good job at a bank but he does not really enjoy his job. Carl often wishes that he had more friends. Somehow he has lost touch with all his old 'buddies': some moved away from Manchester, some got too busy to see him due to family commitments and others just seem to have faded into the background. His friends used to be such a big part of his life, almost like family; he spent most of his birthdays and holidays with them as he has never been close to his real family. Carl has on several occasions wondered if there is something wrong with him as people do not seem to wish to be a permanent part of his life – something that has to date also been applicable to the girlfriends he has had. None of his relationships has lasted longer than six months and it is now over two years since he had a girlfriend.

Because Carl has a good job and is single, he has a high disposable income. He drives a Mercedes, likes to dress in Armani suits, and has a particular love for computer games and gadgets. His latest pride and joy is a big flat-screen plasma TV. He has told all his colleagues and neighbours about his new television. Sometimes he looks at others and thinks that they must be very unfortunate since they do not appear to be able to afford nice things, and he also thinks that he is pretty lucky in that he can buy almost anything he wants, which he does. Carl has, for as long as he can remember, thought that it is important to buy goods that others, especially women, will perceive in a positive light.

Around six months ago Carl increasingly experienced feelings of downheartedness. He could not put his finger on why this was and decided to go to see his GP. His GP diagnosed Carl as being depressed and prescribed him anti-depressants. He also recommended Carl go and see a psychotherapist, which he did. After several sessions the psychotherapist explained to him that she thought that the underlying reason for Carl's depression was linked to the lack of close social relationships and how he instead seemed to put more effort into acquiring new material possessions than making friends. He has since tried very hard not to focus so much on purchasing what he thinks are desirable products but instead has concentrated on how to build up a social support network. He has had some success in doing so but still has a long way to go. However, the feelings of downheartedness have decreased and he hopes that they will disappear altogether once he has made some good close friends.

## TO THINK ABOUT:

1. Is it unethical for marketers to suggest that consumption makes you happy?
2. Can the consumer society in which we live be blamed for people being materialistic?

## FURTHER READING THAT MAY BE OF INTEREST:

If you wish to read more about consumption and how it is linked to well-being, you may wish to read the following:
- Kasser, T., & Kanner, A.D. (Eds.) (2000). *Psychology and consumer culture: The struggle for a good life in a materialistic world*. Washington, DC: American Psychological Association.
- Kasser, T. (2002). *The high price of materialism*. Cambridge, MA: MIT Press.

## FILMS:

You may wish to watch the following docu-comedy produced by Morgan Spurlock:
- *What would Jesus buy?* (2006).

## USEFUL WEBSITES:

It is difficult to find good web resources that directly or indirectly tackle this chapter topic. However, I would recommend you conduct a few Google searches as you are likely to stumble across something that you can explore further.

# 7

# When Shopping Becomes a Burden

For some people, shopping and consumption are not just a frivolous and relatively harmless activity. Instead it can become an uncontrollable disorder, which is what happens when people become 'compulsive buyers' and 'hoarders'. It is only recently that psychologists have started showing interest in those who have an irresistible urge to gather material possessions. Although both disorders have been around for some time, they have become more prominently featured in both academic work and the popular press since the 1980s. The urgency of recognising the psychological conditions has become evident by the suggestion that hoarding be included in the next *Diagnostic and Statistical Manual* (DSM), which is due to be released in 2013 (American Psychiatric Association, 2010). Unfortunately, compulsive buying is yet to be recognised by the DSM, even though several have argued that it should be classified as an impulse control disorder (Faber, 2003).

This chapter will focus mainly on compulsive buying as it is more closely linked to consumption in general.

## Compulsive buying and hoarding

Compulsive buying can be defined as frequent excessive purchasing (Faber, 2003), whilst hoarding is when people are motivated to accumulate obsolete items and are reluctant to dispose of possessions (Cherrier & Ponnor, 2010). Engaging in compulsive buying and hoarding can be very difficult for individuals. Compulsive buying is an impulse control disorder (Black, Repertinger, Gaffney, & Gabel, 1998) and is in some respects similar to hoarding in that impulse control is a feature of both disorders. That is not to say that all compulsive buyers suffer from compulsive hoarding (Mueller et al., 2007). Both disorders, to some extent, resemble obsessive-compulsive disorder (OCD) (e.g. Christenson et al., 1994). In particular, one of the shared features between OCD and compulsive buying is that they more commonly occur in women than in men (Christenson et al., 1994; Karno & Golding, 1991).

It is not known how many people suffer from compulsive buying or hoarding, but some believe that it is prevalent and it may be just as common as OCD, which has been estimated to affect 2–3% of the population (e.g. Christenson et al., 1994). Compulsive buying and hoarding are not exactly the same as OCD but there are a lot of similarities, such as that people with both conditions suffer from irrational and uncontrollable thoughts, and engage in repetitive behaviours that they feel they have to do. They are very much aware that hoarding and purchasing huge amounts of possessions is inappropriate but they simply cannot stop themselves (Christenson et al., 1994).

## Compulsive buying

Compulsive buying behaviour is nothing new; it was originally discussed by Kraepelin (1915) and Bleuler (1924), and both stated that it was a pointless act that often led to serious debt. The clinical term for having a need to gather vast quantities of possessions is acquisitive desire (AD), and one form of AD is compulsive buying. It has been estimated that there may be over half a million people in the UK alone who suffer from compulsive buying behaviour, a behaviour that is also commonly referred to as being a 'shopaholic' (Black, 1996).

Currently there are several definitions of what compulsive buying is. Even though most are relatively similar, there is one difference in that some include both shopping and purchasing (Goldsmith & McElroy, 2000), whilst others propose that the key aspect is the act of buying (Black, 2000; O'Guinn & Faber, 1989). One definition of compulsive buying is that it 'becomes very difficult to stop and ultimately results in harmful consequences' (Faber & O'Guinn, 1992, p.459), demonstrating that it is an involuntary and destructive type of behaviour. This is also something that most researchers within the area seem to agree with. Researchers have gradually sought to establish key aspects of what it means to be a compulsive buyer (e.g. Faber & O'Guinn, 1992; O'Guinn & Faber, 1989), and from such attempts a pattern has emerged.

Both men and women can become addicted to buying. However, research has found that compulsive buying disorder most commonly occurs in women aged between 18 and 30 (e.g. Christenson et al., 1994; Mitchell et al., 2002). There does not appear to be a clear pattern to how often people engage in excessive buying behaviours; it can vary from every day to once every week or month. However, on average it seems that most people experience urges to purchase two or three times a week (Christenson et al., 1994; Schlosser, Black, Repertinger, & Freet, 1994). The commonality between compulsive shoppers is that they all make multiple shopping trips, spend a lot of time and money on purchasing things, and often buy several identical products for no apparent reason.

Compulsive buyers commonly describe their condition as being out of control, distressing and time-consuming (DeSarbo & Edwards, 1996; McElroy, Keck, Pope, Smith, & Strakowski, 1994; O'Guinn & Faber, 1989). Even though most also report some sort of relief whilst engaging in the act of buying, people addicted to shopping often feel slightly depressed and disgusted with themselves just after making a purchase (Riddy, 2000). Unfortunately, the negative feelings they experience afterwards are not enough to deter them from making yet another purchase, as the pre-purchase feelings are strong and make them feel tense and the only way to relieve such tension seems to be through purchasing (Christenson et al., 1994; McElroy et al., 1994).

It has also been found that compulsive buyers tend to suffer from low self-esteem (O'Guinn & Faber, 1989), which may lead to anxiousness and depression (e.g. Faber, 2003; Higgins, 1987).

## How prevalent is the condition?

As already mentioned, it is not known for certain how many people suffer from compulsive buying behaviour. However, that compulsive buying behaviour is prevalent in society was recently noted in a telephone survey where 2,513 American adults were interviewed about buying attitudes and behaviours (Koran, Faber, Aboujaoude, Large, & Serpe, 2006). It was then found that 5.8% of all those interviewed showed clear symptoms of compulsive buying behaviour. If such a sample were representative of the US population then there would currently be somewhere in the region of 17 million people suffering from compulsive buying behaviour. This is a vast number of individuals that may potentially suffer from an illness that is still not always taken seriously (Faber, 2003).

## Downward spiral of consumption

Compulsive buying sufferers tend to continue to shop regardless of how detrimental it may be to them. Often it is only when something goes seriously wrong in their lives that they admit to having a problem (Faber, 2003). Destructive consequences of compulsive buying include embezzlement, suicide attempts, deteriorating mental health, dwindling social relationships and bad finances (Christenson et al., 1994; d'Astous, 1990; Dittmar, 2004; Faber, O'Guinn, & Krych, 1987; O'Guinn & Faber, 1989). Getting into debt seems to be a particularly common problem for those suffering from compulsive buying as research has found that what they spend is not in any way related to their actual income (Faber et al., 1987; Scherhorn, Reisch, & Raab, 1990). The amount of debt they get into is also likely to be worse due to the fact that most Westerners have relatively easy access to credit, which means that they can spend far more than they can afford (Drentea & Lavrakas, 2000; Hatcher, 1994).

## Why do some people become addicted to shopping?

There is no simple answer as to why some consumers become addicted to shopping. So far, there is one common correlate to being a shopping-addicted consumer that consistently features in research literature, and that is materialistic value orientations (d'Astous, 1990; Mowen & Spears, 1999; Yurchisin & Johnson, 2004). The more materialistic an individual is, the more likely they are to become a compulsive consumer, which may suggest that the value they put on possessions can be an underlying cause in why they become addicted. However, this is by no means certain, even though it has repeatedly been established that there is a link between mental disorders and high materialistic value orientations. For example, Cohen and Cohen (1996) found that teenagers who admire people based on their possessions are more likely to develop personality disorders.

It has also been suggested that the consumer society is to blame (Elliott, 1994) in that easy access to credit cards encourages over-consumption (Boundy, 2000).

## Childhood experiences

Compulsive consumption may partially be the result of experiences that individuals have during their childhood (Walls & Smith, 1970). For example, it has been found that young adults who have been brought up in households where parents are separated or divorced are more likely to engage in compulsive consumption than those reared in two-parent families (Rindfleisch et al., 1997). The question is why children in one-parent families are more prone to becoming addicted to shopping. There appear to be several feasible explanations, such as that material possessions may function as a substitute for close personal relationships (Belk, 1985; Richins, 1994). Children may simply become worried about getting close to others in case they leave them. Instead, they may find that hugging their favourite teddy bear gives them some sort of comfort. The idea that material possessions can be comforting is then transferred into adulthood, when it may become harder and harder to establish close social relationships due to having avoided them for so long.

Low self-esteem is also a factor that probably plays a part in why people become more likely to engage in compulsive consumption (Richins & Dawson, 1992). Young adults often experience feelings of insecurity due to the stressful conditions they are subjected to when their parents separate (An, Haveman, & Wolfe, 1993). One way of dealing with such feelings is to show that they are 'in charge' of possessions. Other factors include being unhappy with one's life, as well as wishing that one had a higher income (Richins & Dawson, 1992), also reflecting life as a child in a single-parent family.

It has been suggested that compulsive buyers are often perfectionists (e.g. DeSarbo & Edwards, 1996) and that the perfectionism may have been brought on by parental expectations. The compulsive behaviour can then be a way to show their parents that they are not perfect (Faber, 2003).

## Connection between narcissism and compulsive buying

Childhood influences may also be indirectly linked to compulsive buying through narcissistic personality characteristics. Narcissistic tendencies can be the consequence of parents failing to foster healthy self-esteem in their young children (Kohut & Wolf, 1978). Children's self-esteem is easily reinforced through simple actions such as praise. However, if parents fail to let their children know that they have done something well it is likely to knock their confidence. For those with narcissistic personality characteristics it is likely that their parents may repeatedly have failed to reinforce their self-esteem by putting their own needs first. An example of how parents may put their own needs before the needs of their child can be noted in the following:

> A little girl comes home from school, eager to tell her mother about some great successes. But this mother, instead of listening with pride, deflects the conversation from the child to herself [and] begins to talk about her own successes which overshadow those of her little daughter. (Kohut & Wolf, 1978, p.418)

Researchers have found a link between narcissism and compulsive buying (Rose, 2007). Since narcissists engage in egoistical behaviours (Morf & Rhodewalt, 2001), it is believed that underlying reasons for compulsive buying may be associated with their desire to be admired by others (Campbell & Foster, 2007; Morf & Rhodewalt, 2001). For example, a narcissist may think that if they drive an expensive sports car, other people will look at them with envy. It may also be possible to explain the correlation between narcissism and compulsive buying by looking at a narcissist's lack of personal restraints (Rose, 2007). Narcissism has previously been linked to poor impulse control, and narcissists have been found at a young age to be more likely to be heavy drinkers (Luhtanen & Crocker, 2005) and sexually promiscuous (Foster, Shrira, & Campbell, 2006). The inability to regulate one's own behaviour has also been linked to a string of other addictive behaviours such as alcohol use (Granö, Virtanen, Vahtera, Elovainio, & Kivimäki, 2004), problem gambling (Clarke, 2006) and Ecstasy use (Butler & Montgomery, 2004). Hence, it may be that failure to refrain from engaging in certain behaviours is the common factor between narcissism and compulsive buying behaviour.

## The role of emotions

Another theory in regard to why consumers engage in compulsive buying behaviour is linked to the way people are feeling. It has been suggested that individuals overconsume in the hope of forgetting about something in particular, such as a negative life event, some sort of deficiency or maybe negative feelings (O'Guinn & Faber, 1989; Scherhorn et al., 1990). The idea is that the compulsive behaviour works as some sort of relief from negative emotions so that they forget about them, even if it is only momentarily.

That emotions play some part in why people engage in compulsive buying was found when Faber and O'Guinn (1992) interviewed 24 compulsive buyers. From these interviews it was established that they were more likely to buy things when they felt angry, lonely, frustrated, hurt or irritable. It was also found that the buying episode itself acted as a catalyst for those feelings and consequently they experienced more positive emotions and felt less tense than they had previously done. The idea that compulsive buying offers some sort of relief to the individual concerned suggests similarities to other disorders such as binge eating (e.g. Stickney, Miltenberger, & Wolff, 1999), where bingeing on food makes people temporarily forget about their worries.

## How to cure compulsive buying

Compulsive buying is an illness and it needs to be treated as such. Since compulsive buying is not included in the manual (DSM IV) used to diagnose mental illnesses (American Psychiatric Association, 1994) there are no diagnostic criteria. There may be several reasons as to why compulsive buying is yet to be included in the DSM, but two in particular spring to mind. First, it is yet to be established whether compulsive buying is a disorder that occurs across the globe. It is possible that it is found only in industrialised societies where consumption is an integral part of society (Babbar, 2007). To date there have been few cross-cultural studies investigating the phenomena of compulsive buying behaviour and those that exist have been done between countries where consumption is indeed part of everyday life (e.g. Kwak, Zinkhan, & Crask, 2003). Until it has been clearly established that compulsive behaviour is a genuine cross-cultural illness, it is unlikely that it will be included in the next diagnostic manual for mental disorders.

The second reason is likely to be linked to the fact that there are numerous theories as to what kind of illness compulsive buying is. So far it has been likened to impulse control disorder (Christenson et al., 1994; McElroy, Keck, & Phillips, 1995), mood disorders (Lejoyeyx, Tassian, Solomon, & Adés, 1997), addiction (Scherhorn, 1990) and obsessive-compulsive disorder (Hollander, 1993). How the disorder ought to be classified is an ongoing debate, one that does not seem likely to be resolved any time soon.

Even though compulsive buying is not included in DSM IV, attempts have been made to establish what symptoms clinical psychologists should look out for when diagnosing patients, as well as what treatments should be used. General symptoms of being a compulsive buyer include regularly thinking about buying, spending excessive amounts of time shopping, experiencing strong urges to buy, and spending more than one can afford. Those symptoms in conjunction with some sort of adverse experiences such as serious financial problems or diminishing social relationships are generally clear indicators that a person is suffering from compulsive buying behaviour (McElroy et al., 1994). Taking aspects such as those mentioned previously into account the Compulsive Buying Scale was developed as a tool for diagnosing compulsive buying behaviour (Faber & O'Guinn, 1992). It is currently the most commonly used tool for diagnosing individuals who suffer from the disorder. The Compulsive Buying Scale was devised using an American sample to establish the seven items that the scale consists of. Because the scale was created using only US participants it is possible that it is culture-specific (e.g. Kwak et al., 2003).

## Overlapping symptoms

One difficulty that clinical practitioners may be faced with is that compulsive buyers often display symptoms of other psychopathological disorders in parallel with their compulsive buying behaviour, such as substance abuse (Christenson et al., 1994) and eating disorders (McElroy et al., 1995; Mitchell et al., 2002). This can make it difficult for them to diagnose what the problem is. Hence, it has been suggested that therapists may on occasion treat the other apparent symptoms without realising that the client is suffering from compulsive buying disorder (Kottler, Montgomery, & Shepard, 2003).

Because of its similarities and associations to other disorders, treatment of compulsive buying disorder has so far been the same as it would be for the other disorders. Thus a mixture of talking and biologically based therapies has been used.

The medication used to cure AD sufferers (e.g. Black, Monahan, & Gabel, 1997; Grant, 2003; Lejoyeux, Hourtané, & Adés, 1995) has yet to be conclusively proven to be a sufficient way to cure compulsive buying behaviours (Mitchell, Burgard, Faber, Crosby, & de Zwaan, 2006).

## Treatment plan

A general treatment plan that can be applied to compulsive buying behaviour has been developed (Kottler & Stevens, 1999). The plan requires that the therapist have a solid collaborative relationship with their client. Once such a connection has been established the treatment can be implemented in whatever order the therapist thinks will suit the client best. The overall idea is that together the client and therapist will explore different aspects that are directly or indirectly linked to the disorder, such as the cultural context, maladaptive thought processes, how to deal with guilt and how to replace the undesired behaviour itself. The treatment plan is particularly useful in that it can be utilised by therapists with different theoretical orientations (Kottler et al., 2003). So far little research has been conducted to test if different types of therapies are more or less effective when it comes to treating compulsive buying disorder.

## The use of Cognitive Behavioural Therapy

Recent studies have shown some promising results for the use of Cognitive Behavioural Therapy (CBT) as a treatment method. In a study where 28 compulsive buyers who received CBT were compared against 11 compulsive buyers that had as yet not had any treatment, it was found that CBT can be an effective way of treating compulsive shopping behaviours (Mitchell et al., 2006). Such results indicate that non-medically based therapies can be strong contenders for curing compulsive buyers. However, since most of the published work to date that has looked at using psychotherapy has been in the form of case studies (e.g. Lawrence, 1990), more research is needed in order to prove that it is a genuinely effective treatment method.

## Summary

Shopping is no longer a fun and frivolous activity when people become addicted to it. People are addicted when they find it difficult to stop and when there are negative consequences of engaging in shopping. It has been estimated that compulsive buying behaviour affects around 5% of the population in Westernised societies.

People who value material possessions highly and suffer from low self-esteem appear to be more likely to become addicted to shopping.

Currently, there are no specific diagnostic criteria for addictive shopping, and it can be particularly difficult to diagnose as patients often also display other symptoms such as substance abuse. Several different types of treatment techniques have been used to cure patients who are addicted to shopping, including talking therapies and medication.

## The compulsive buyer

Sarah (please note that the name is fabricated) is 26 years old. She has a good job as a lawyer in London, a nice car and a lovely flat in a desirable part of the city. Her colleagues always think that she is immaculately dressed and only buys designer clothes, and her secretary has on several occasions commented on how envious she is of the Rolex that Sarah would never dream of taking off.

Sarah's favourite pastime is shopping, which she does whenever she has the opportunity: in the morning before work, during her lunch break and on her way home from work. There are days when she needs to be in very early at work, skip lunch and work late, leaving her with no time for shopping. On such days Sarah feels really anxious and is easily agitated. Every time she buys something she feels really excited as if she gets a 'high' from acquiring new things, but that feeling never lasts long and after a while it turns into feelings of guilt for having purchased yet another item that she does not really need. In the last three months she has bought six pairs of shoes, four handbags, a bed sofa, two sets of bed linen, fourteen new CDs, a photo frame, two pairs of sunglasses, two pillows, three paintings, a shredder, a lamp, curtains, a laptop, an iPod, four table cloths, a chair, a kettle, a set of saucepans, two dressing gowns and a camera. This is despite Sarah already owning one or more of most of these items. Her beautiful flat is so full of things that she has bought recently that it is impossible to find somewhere to sit.

Even though Sarah earns a decent amount of money she has a lot of debt. Her two credit cards are maxed out, she has used up her overdraft and she recently borrowed £6,000 from her bank. To make matters worse she has not paid her mortgage for the last two months. All her money is spent shopping and she justifies this to herself by saying that she deserves it as she had very few material possessions as a child. Her mother, who was a cleaner, walked out of the family home when Sarah was 13 and never came back, leaving her alcoholic father to look after her and her two siblings.

Because of Sarah's frivolous spending she is on the brink of bankruptcy and that fact has made her feel depressed.

## TO THINK ABOUT:

1. Can society somehow help prevent people from becoming addicted to shopping?
2. Should shopaholics be treated by the NHS?

## FURTHER READING THAT MAY BE OF INTEREST:

If you wish to read more about compulsive consumers you may want to look at the following two books by April Lane Benson:

- Lane Benson, A. (2008). *To buy or not to buy: Why we overshop and how to stop.* Boston, MA: Trumpeter.
- Lane Benson, A. (2000). *I shop therefore I am: Compulsive buying & the search for self.* Northvale, NJ: Jason Aronson.

## FILMS:

You may wish to watch the short film by Martin Hampton that explores the lives of four people who obsessively collect material possessions:

- *Possessed* (2008).

The film can be seen at: http://consumerist.com/2009/06/documentary-looks-at-compulsive-hoarders.html

## USEFUL WEBSITES:

To learn more about compulsive buying and hoarding you may wish to look at one of the following websites:

- **Compulsive Hoarding:** http://www.compulsivehoarding.org
- **International OCD Foundation:** http://www.ocfoundation.org/hoarding/
- **CNS Spectrums:** http://www.cnsspectrums.com/aspx/articledetail.aspx?articleid=977

# References

Abramovitz, J.N., & Mattoon, A.T. (1999). Reorienting the forest products economy. In L.R. Brown, C. Flavin, H.F. French & L. Starke (Eds.), *State of the world, 1999: A Worldwatch Institute report on progress toward a sustainable society* (pp. 60–77). New York: Worldwatch Institute.

Achenreiner, G.B. (1997). Materialistic values and susceptibility to influence in children. In M. Brooks & D.J. MacInnis (Eds.), *Advances in consumer research*, Vol. 24 (pp. 82–88). Provo, UT: Association for Consumer Research.

AC Nielsen (2007). Beauty and the bucks. Retrieved September 16, 2007 from *http://www.nielsen.com/us/en/insights/press-room/2007/template21.html*

Ahluwalia, R., Burnkrant, R.E., & Unnava, H.R. (2000). Consumer response to negative publicity: The moderating role of commitment. *Journal of Marketing Research*, 37, 203–214.

Ahuvia, A.C. (2002). Individualism/collectivism and cultures of happiness: A theoretical conjecture on the relationship between consumption, culture and subjective well-being at the national level. *Journal of Happiness Studies*, 3, 23–36.

Ahuvia, A.C., & Wong, N. (1998). The effect of cultural orientation in luxury consumption. In E.J. Arnould & L.M. Scott (Eds.), *Advances in Consumer Research* (pp. 29–32). Ann Arbor, MI: Association for Consumer Research.

Ajzen, I. (1988). *Attitudes, personality, and behaviour*. Buckingham, UK: Open University Press.

Alexander, S.J., Weigand, J., & Blatner, K.A. (2002). Nontimber forest product commerce. In E. Jones, R. McLain & L. Weigand (Eds.), *Nontimber forest products in the United States*. Lawrence: University Press of Kansas.

All Business (2007). The NPD group reports U.S. toy industry sales showed increases in 2006. Retrieved December 19, 2007 from *http://www.allbusiness.com/services/business-services/3970448-1.html*

114

Allen, M. (1991). Meta-analysis comparing the persuasiveness of one-sided and two-sided messages. *Western Journal of Speech Communication*, 55, 390–404.

Allison, N.K., Golden, L.L., Mullet, G.M., & Coogan, D. (1979). Sex-typed product images: The effects of sex, sex role self-concept and measurement implications. *Advances in Consumer Research*, 7, 604–609.

Alreck, P.L., Settle, R.B., & Belch, M.A. (1982). Who responds to gendered ads, and how? *Journal of Advertising Research*, 22, 25–32.

American Academy of Pediatrics (2000). Joint statement on the impact of entertainment violence on children, Congressional Public Health Summit, July 26, 2000. Retrieved January 12, 2008 from *http://www.aap.org/advocacy/releases/jstmtevc.htm*

American Academy of Pediatrics Committee on Public Education (2001). Children, adolescents, and television. *Pediatrics*, 107, 423–426.

American Psychiatric Association (1994). *Diagnostic and statistical manual of mental disorders* (4th edition). Washington, DC: Author.

American Psychiatric Association (2010). Retrieved December 5, 2010 from *http://www.dsm5.org/Pages/Default.aspx*

American Society for Aesthetic Plastic Surgery (2005). Cosmetic surgery quick facts: 2005 ASAPS statistics. Retrieved January 10, 2008 from *http://www.surgery.org/press/procedurefacts-asqf.php*

Amin, A., & Thrift, N. (2005). What's left? Just the future. *Antipode*, 37, 220–238.

An, C., Haveman, R., & Wolfe, B. (1993). Teen out-of-wedlock births and welfare receipt: The role of childhood events and economic circumstances. *Review of Economics and Statistics*, 75, 195–208.

Anderson, C.A. (2004). An update on the effects of playing violent video games. *Journal of Adolescence*, 27, 113–122.

Annetta, L. (2010). The 'I's' have it: A framework for serious educational game design. *Review of General Psychology*, 14, 105–112.

Argenti, P.A. (2004). Collaborating with activists: How Starbucks works with NGOs. *California Management Review*, 47, 91–116.

Argyle, M., & McHenry, R. (1971). Do spectacles really affect judgement of intelligence? *British Journal of Social and Clinical Psychology*, 10, 27–29.

Arkin, R.M., & Maruyama, G.M. (1979). Attribution, affect, and college exam performance. *Journal of Educational Psychology*, 71, 85–93.

Arriaga, P., Esteves, F., Carneiro, P., & Monteiro, M.B. (2006). Violent computer games and their effects on state hostility and physiological arousal. *Aggressive Behavior*, 32, 358–371.

Arvola, A., Vassallo, M., Dean, M., Lampila, P., Saba, A., Lahteenmaki, R., & Shepherd, R. (2008). Predicting intentions to purchase organic food: The role of affective and moral attitudes in the Theory of Planned Behaviour. *Appetite, 50,* 443–454.

Atran, S., Medin, D.L., & Ross, N.O. (2005). The cultural mind: Environmental decision making and cultural modelling within and across populations. *Psychological Review,* 112, 744–776.

Auger, P., Burke, P., Devinney, T.M., & Louviere, J.J. (2003). What will consumers pay for social product features? *Journal of Business Ethics,* 42, 281–304.

Auger, P., Burke, P., Devinney, T.M., & Louviere, J.J. (2004a). Consumer assessment of social product features: An empirical investigation using choice experiments. Unpublished working paper.

Auger, P., Burke, P., Devinney, T.M., & Louviere, J.J. (2004b). Consumer social beliefs: An international investigation using best-worst scaling methodology. Unpublished working paper.

Auger, P., & Devinney, T.M. (2007). Do what consumers say matter? The misalignment of preferences with unconstrained ethical intentions. *Journal of Business Ethics,* 76, 361–383.

Babbar, J. (2007). Correspondence. Compulsive buying: A culture bound disorder? *International Journal of Social Psychiatry,* 53, 189.

Bagnall, D. (1996). Beauty and the beasts. *The Bulletin,* October 29, pp. 16–19.

Ball, K., Crawford, D., & Kenardy, J. (2004). Longitudinal relationships among overweight, life satisfaction, and aspirations in young women. *Obesity Research,* 12, 1019–1030.

Bandura, A. (1977). *Social learning theory.* New York: General Learning Press.

Bandura, A. (1986). *Social foundations of thought and action: A social cognitive theory.* Englewood Cliffs, NJ: Prentice-Hall.

Bandura, A. (2002). Social cognitive theory of mass communication. In J. Bryant and D. Zillman (Eds.), *Media effects: Advances in theory and research* (2nd edition) (pp. 121–153). Mahwah, NJ: Lawrence Erlbaum.

Barcus, F.E. (1980). The nature of television advertising to children. In E. Palmer & A. Dorr (Eds.), *Children and the faces of television* (pp. 273–285). New York: Academic Press.

Barnett, C., Cloke, P., Clarke, N., & Malpass, A. (2005). Consuming ethics: Articulating the subjects and spaces of ethical consumption. *Antipode,* 37, 24–45.

Barnett, C., Cloke, P., Clarke, N., & Malpass, A. (2006). The subjects and spaces of ethical consumption: Doing politics in an ethical register. Retrieved November 25, 2007 from *http://www.consume.bbk.ac.uk/researchfindings/ethical.pdf*

Bartky, S.L. (2003). Foucault, femininity and the modernization of patriarchal power. In R. Weitz (Ed.), *The politics of women's bodies:*

*Sexuality, appearance, and behavior* (pp. 25–45). New York: Oxford University Press.

Bassili, J N. (1996). Meta-judgemental versus operative indexes of psychological attributes: The case of measures of attitude strength. *Journal of Personality and Social Psychology*, 71, 637–653.

Baudrillard, J. (1998). *The consumer society.* London: Sage.

BBC News (2000). Gap and Nike: No sweat? Retrieved December 3, 2007 from *http://news.bbc.co.uk/1/hi/programmes/panorama/970385.stm*

BBC News (2007). Nip'n'tuck loans offer in Lebanon. Retrieved October 5, 2007 from *http://news.bbc.co.uk/1/hi/world/middle_east/6577497.stm*

Bearden, W.O., & Rose, R.L. (1990). Attention to social comparison information: An individual difference factor affecting consumer conformity. *Journal of Consumer Research*, 16, 461–471.

Becker, A.E., Burwell, R.A., Gilman, S.E., Herzog, D.B., & Hamburg, P. (2002). Eating behaviours and attitudes following prolonged exposure to television among ethnic Fijian adolescent girls. *British Journal of Psychiatry*, 180, 509–514.

Beentjes, J.W.J., Koolstra, C.M., Marseille, N., & van der Voort, T.H. (2001). Children's use of different media: For how long and why? In S. Livingstone and M. Bovill (Eds.), *Children and their changing media environment: A European comparative study* (pp. 85–112). Mahwah, NJ: Lawrence Erlbaum.

Belk, R.W. (1978). Assessing the effects of visible consumption on impression formation. In H.K. Hunt & A. Arbor (Eds.), *Advances in Consumer Research*, 5 (pp. 39–47). Ann Arbor, MI: Association for Consumer Research.

Belk, R.W. (1985). Materialism: Trait aspects of living in the material world. *Journal of Consumer Research*, 12, 265–280.

Belk, R.W. (1988). Possessions and the extended self. *Journal of Consumer Research*, 15, 139–168.

Belk, R.W. (2000). Are we what we own? In A. Benson (Ed.), *I shop therefore I am: Compulsive buying and the search for self* (pp. 76–104). New York: Jason Aronson.

Belk, R. (2006). Consumption, mass consumption, and consumer culture. In G. Ritzer (Ed.), *Blackwell encyclopedia of sociology.* Oxford: Blackwell.

Belk, R.W., Devinney, T.M., & Eckhardt, G. (2005). Consumer ethics across cultures. *Consumption, Markets and Culture*, 8, 275–289.

Benight, C.C., Ironson, G., Klebe, K., Carver, C.S., Wynings, C., Burnett, K., Greenwood, D., Baum, A., & Schneiderman, N. (1999). Conservation of resources and coping self-efficacy predicting distress following a natural disaster: A causal model analysis where the environment meets the mind. *Anxiety, Stress & Coping: An International Journal*, 12, 107–126.

Benson, A. (Ed.) (2000). *I shop, therefore I am: Compulsive buying and the search for self*. New York: Jason Aronson.

Berkes, F., Feeny, D., McCay, B., & Acheson, J. (1989). The benefit of the commons. *Nature*, 340, 91–93.

Berkowitz, L. (1972). Social norms, feelings, and other factors affecting helping and altruism. In L. Berkowitz (Ed.), *Advances in experimental social psychology*, Vol. 6 (pp. 63–108). San Diego, CA: Academic Press.

Bernard-Bonnin, A.C., Gilbert, S., Rousseau, E., Masson, P., & Maheux, B. (1991). Television and the 3- to 10-year-old child. *Pediatrics*, 88, 48–53.

Berry, B. (2008). *The power of looks: Social stratification of physical appearance*. Aldershot, UK: Ashgate.

Berry, G.L. (2000). Multicultural media portrayals and the changing demographic landscape: The psychosocial impact of television representations on the adolescent of color. *Journal of Adolescent Health*, 27, 57–60.

Bessenoff, G.R. (2006). Can the media affect us? Social comparison, self-discrepancy, and the thin ideal. *Psychology of Women Quarterly*, 30, 239–251.

Bickman, L. (1971). The effect of social status on the honesty of others. *Journal of Social Psychology*, 85, 87–92.

Birch, L.L., Johnson, S.L., & Fisher, J.A. (1995). Children's eating: The development of food acceptance patterns. *Young Children*, 50, 71–78.

Bisignani, G. (2011). State of the industry speech. Retrieved June 12, 2011 from *http://www.iata.org/pressroom/speeches/Pages/2011-06-06-01.aspx*

Black, D.W. (1996). Compulsive buying. *Journal of Clinical Psychiatry*, 57, 50–54.

Black, D.W. (2000). Assessment of compulsive buying. In A.L. Benson (Ed.), *I shop, therefore I am: Compulsive buying and the search for self* (pp. 191–216). New York: Jason Aronson.

Black, D.W., Monahan, P., & Gabel, J. (1997). Fluvoxamine in the treatment of compulsive buying. *Journal of Clinical Psychiatry*, 58, 159–163.

Black, D.W., Repertinger, S., Gaffney, G.R., & Gabel, J. (1998). Family history and psychiatric comorbidity in persons with compulsive buying: Preliminary findings. *American Journal of Psychiatry*, 155, 960–963.

Black, J.S., Stern, P.C., & Elworth, J.T. (1985). Personal and contextual influences on household energy adaptations. *Journal of Applied Psychology*, 70, 3–21.

Black, R.E., Morris, S.S., & Bryce, J. (2003). Where and why are 10 million children dying every year? *Lancet*, 361, 2226–2234.

Blanton, H., Buunk, B.P., Gibbons, F.X., & Kuyper, H. (1999). When better-than-others compare upward: Choice of comparison and comparative evaluation as independent predictors of academic performance. *Journal of Personality and Social Psychology*, 76, 420–430.

Bleuler, E. (1924). *Textbook of psychiatry*. New York: Macmillan.

Bomford, A. (2006). Slow death of Africa's Lake Chad. Retrieved April 14, 2006 from *http://news.bbc.co.uk/1/hi/4906692.stm*

Boot, W., Kramer, A., Simons, D., Fabiani, M., & Gratton, G. (2008). The effects of video game playing on attention, memory and executive control. *Acta Psychologica*, 129, 387–398.

Borah, G., Rankin, M., & Wey, P. (1999). Psychological complications in 281 plastic surgery practices. *Plastic and Reconstructive Surgery*, 104, 1241–1246.

Boundy, D. (2000). When money is the drug. In A.L. Benson (Ed.), *I shop, therefore I am: Compulsive buying and the search for self* (pp. 3–26). Northvale, NJ: Jason Aronson.

Braun, O.L., & Wicklund, R.A. (1989). Psychological antecedents of conspicuous consumption. *Journal of Economic Psychology*, 10, 161–187.

Bray, G.A. (1998). *Contemporary diagnosis and management of obesity*. Newton, PA: Handbooks in Health Care.

Brenton, S., & ten Hacken, L. (2006). Ethical consumerism: Are unethical labour practices important to consumers? *Journal of Research for Consumers*, 11, 1–11.

Brickman, P., & Campbell, D.T. (1971). Hedonic relativism and planning the good society. In M.H. Apley (Ed.), *Adaptation-level theory: A symposium* (pp. 287–302). New York: Academic Press.

British Toy and Hobby Association (2007). UK toy industry worth £2.2 billion after strong performance in 2006. Retrieved October 5, 2007 from *http://www.btha.co.uk/press/industry_worth.php?PHPSESSID =edfb519a1697e943767e86abdbd0e181*

Brower, M., & Leon, W. (1999). *The consumer's guide to effective environmental choices: Practical advice from the Union of Concerned Scientists*. New York: Three Rivers Press.

Brown, A., Furnham, A., Glanville, L., & Swami, V. (2007). Factors that affect the likelihood of undergoing cosmetic surgery. *Aesthetic Surgery Journal*, 27, 501–508.

Brown, J.D., Childers, K., Bauman, K., & Koch, G. (1990). The influence of new media and family structure on young adolescents' television and radio use. *Communication Research*, 17, 65–82.

Brown, M. (2009). Leading ladies kept out of the limelight. *Guardian*, June 17, p. 9.

Brown, S. (1995). *Post modern marketing*. London: Routledge.

Bushman, B.J., & Anderson, C.A. (2001). Media violence and the American public: Scientific facts versus media misinformation. *American Psychologist, 56*, 477–489.

Bushman, B.J., & Huesmann, L.R. (2001). Effects of televised violence on aggression. In D.G. Singer & J.L. Singer (Eds.), *Handbook of children and the media* (pp. 223–254). Thousand Oaks, CA: Sage.

Buss, D.M. (2000). The evolution of happiness. *American Psychologist, 55*, 15–23.

Butler, G.K.L., & Montgomery, A.M.J. (2004). Impulsivity, risk taking and recreational 'Ecstasy' (MDMA) use. *Drug and Alcohol Dependence, 76*, 55–62.

Calogero, R.M., Boroughs, M., & Thompson, J.K. (2007). The impact of western beauty ideals on the lives of women and men: A sociocultural perspective. In V. Swami & A. Furnham (Eds.), *Body beautiful: Evolutionary and sociocultural perspectives* (pp. 259–298). New York: Palgrave Macmillan.

Calogero, R.M., Herbozo, S., & Thompson, J.K. (2009). Complimentary weightism: The potential costs of appearance-related commentary for women's self-objectification. *Psychology of Women Quarterly, 33*, 120–132.

Campbell, W.K., & Foster, J.D. (2007). The narcissistic self: Background, an extended agency model, and ongoing controversies. In C. Sedikides & S. Spencer (Eds.), *Frontier in social psychology: The self* (pp. 115–138). Philadelphia, PA: Psychology Press.

Campfield, L.A., Smith, F.J., Guisez, Y., Devos, R., & Burn, P. (1995). Recombinant mouse OB protein: Evidence for a peripheral signal linking adiposity and central neural networks. *Science, 269*, 546–549.

Cardon, L.R. (1994). Height, weight, and obesity. In J.C. DeFries, R. Plomin & D.W. Fulker (Eds.), *Nature and nurture during middle childhood*. Oxford: Blackwell.

Carrigan, M., & Attalla, A. (2001). The myth of the ethical consumer: Do ethics matter in purchase behavior? *Journal of Consumer Marketing, 7*, 560–577.

Carvel, J. (2006). Child obesity has doubled in a decade: Junk food and lack of exercise have created 'public health timebomb'. *Guardian*, April 22. Retrieved September 18, 2006 from *http://www.guardian.co.uk/society/2006/apr/22/health.schools*

Cash, T.F., Duel, L.A., & Perkins, L.L. (2002). Women's psychosocial outcomes of breast augmentation with silicone gel-filled implants: A two-year prospective study. *Plastic and Reconstructive Surgery, 109*, 2112–2121.

Castel, A., Pratt, J., & Drummond, E. (2005). The effects of action video game experience on the time course of inhibition of return and the efficiency of visual search. *Acta Psychologica, 119*, 217–230.

Chagnon, Y.C., Perusse, L., Weisnagel, S.J., Rankinen, T., & Bouchard, C. (2000). The human obesity gene map: The 1999 update. *Obesity Research*, 8, 89–117.

Chan, R., & Joseph, S. (2000). Dimensions of personality, domains of aspiration, and subjective well-being. *Personality and Individual Differences*, 28, 347–354.

Chandler, T.N., & Heinzerling, B.M. (1999). *Children and adolescents in the market place: Twenty-five years of academic research.* Ann Arbor, MI: Pierian.

Chang, L.C., & Arkin, R.M. (2002). Materialism as an attempt to cope with uncertainty. *Psychology and Marketing*, 19, 389–406.

Chatzidakis, A., Hibbert, S., Mittusis, D., & Smith, A. (2004). Virtue in consumption? *Journal of Marketing Management*, 20, 527–544.

Chatzidakis, A., Hibbert, S., & Smith, A. (2007). Why people don't take their concerns about fair trade to the supermarket: The role of neutralisation. *Journal of Business Ethics*, 74, 89–100.

Cheadle, A., Psaty, B., Curry, S., Wagner, E., Diehr, P., Koepsell, T., & Kristal, A. (1991). Community-level comparisons between the grocery store environment and individual dietary practices. *Preventative Medicine*, 20, 250–261.

Cheadle, A., Psaty, B., Diehr, P., Koepsell, T., Wagner, E., Curry, S., & Kristal, A. (1995). Evaluating community-based nutrition programs: Comparing grocery store and individual-level survey measures of program impact. *Preventative Medicine*, 24, 71–79.

Cherrier, H., & Ponnor, T. (2010). A study of hoarding behavior and attachment to material possessions. *Journal of Qualitative Market Research*, 13, 8–23.

Christenson, G.A., Faber, R.J., de Zwaan, M., Raymond, N.C., Specker, S.M., Ekern, M.D., et al. (1994). Compulsive buying: Descriptive characteristics and psychiatric comorbidity. *Journal of Clinical Psychiatry*, 55, 5–11.

Cialdini, R.B., Reno, R.R., & Kallgren, C.A. (1990). A focus theory of normative conduct: Recycling the concept of social norms to reduce littering in public places. *Journal of Personality and Social Psychology*, 58, 1015–1026.

Cialdini, R.B., Wosinska, W., Barrett, D.W., Butner, J., & Gornik-Durose, M. (1999). Compliance with a request in two cultures: The differential influence of social proof and commitment/consistency on collectivists and individualists. *Personality and Social Psychology Bulletin*, 25, 1242–1253.

Citrin, J., Wong, C., & Duff, B. (2001). The meaning of American national identity. In R. Ashmore, L. Jussim, & D. Wilder (Eds.), *Social identity, intergroup conflict, and conflict reduction* (pp. 71–100). New York: Oxford University Press.

Clarke, D. (2006). Impulsivity as a mediator in the relationship between depression and problem gambling. *Personality and Individual Differences*, 40, 5–15.

Clayton, S., & Brook, A. (2005). Can psychology help save the world? A model for conservation psychology. *Analyses of Social Issues and Public Policy*, 5, 1–15.

Clements, D.H., & Nastasi, B.K. (1992). Computers and early childhood education. In M. Gettinger, S.N. Elliott & T.R. Kratochwill (Eds.), *Advances in school psychology: Preschool and early childhood treatment directions* (pp. 187–246). Hillsdale, NJ: Lawrence Erlbaum.

Clifford, B.R., Gunter, B., & McAleer, J. (1995). *Program evaluation, comprehension and impact.* Hillsdale, NJ: Lawrence Erlbaum.

Cohen, P., & Cohen, J. (1996). *Life values and adolescent mental health.* Mahwah, NJ: Lawrence Erlbaum.

Cole, K.N., Mills, P.E., Dale, P.S., & Jenkins, J.R. (1991). Effects of preschool integration for children with disabilities. *Exceptional Children*, 58, 36–45.

Collins, W.A., Sobol, S.K., & Westby, S. (1981). Effects of adult commentary on children's comprehension and inferences about a televised aggressive portrayal. *Child Development*, 52, 158–163.

Collis, B.A. (1996). *Children and computers at school.* Mahwah, NJ: Lawrence Erlbaum.

Committee of Inquiry into Cosmetic Surgery (1999). *The cosmetic surgery report: Report to the NSW Minister for Health, October 1999.* Strawberry Hills, Australia: NSW Health Care Commission.

Comstock, G. (1991). *Television and the American child.* San Diego, CA: Academic Press.

Condry, J., Bence, P., & Scheibe, C. (1988). Nonprogram content of children's television. *Journal of Broadcasting*, 32, 255–270.

Condry, J.C., & Freund, S. (1989). Discriminating real from make-believe: A developmental study. Paper presented at the biennial meeting of the Society for Research in Child Development, Kansas City.

Cone, J.D., & Hayes, S.C. (1980). *Environmental problems/behavioral solutions.* Monterey, CA: Brooks/Cole.

Conners, N., Tripathi, S., Clubb, R., & Bradley, R. (2007). Maternal characteristics associated with television viewing habits of low-income preschool children. *Journal of Child and Family Studies*, 16, 415–425.

Consulting Room (2007). 2006 BAAPS: Over 28,900 cosmetic surgery procedures in the UK in 2006. Retrieved August 24, 2007 from *http://www.consultingroom.com/Statistics/Display.asp?Statistics_ID=22&Title=2006%20BAAPS:%20Over%2028,900%20Cosmetic%20Surgery%20Procedures%20in%20The%20UK%20in%202006*

Cooper, H., Schembri, S., & Miller, D. (2010). Brand-self identity narratives in the James Bond movies. *Psychology and Marketing*, 27, 557–567.

Cooper-Martin, E., & Holbrook, M.B. (1993). Ethical consumption experiences and ethical space. *Advances in Consumer Research*, 20, 113–118.

Costanzo, M., Archer, D., Aronson, E., & Pettigrew, T. (1986). Energy conservation behavior: The difficult path from information to action. *American Psychologist*, 41, 521–528.

Cragg, A., Taylor, C., & Toombs, B. (2007). Video games: Research to improve understanding of what players enjoy about video games, and to explain their preferences for particular games. London: British Board of Film Classification. Retrieved from *http://www.bbfc.co.uk*

Crandall, C.S. (1994). Prejudice against fat people: Ideology and self-interest. *Journal of Personality and Social Psychology*, 66, 882–894.

Crane, A. (2001). Unpacking the ethical product. *Journal of Business Ethics*, 30, 361–373.

Crespo, C.J., Smit, E., Troiano, R., Bartlett, S.J., Macera, C.A., & Andersen, R.E. (2001). Television watching, energy intake, and obesity in U.S. children: Results from the third national health and nutrition examination survey, 1988–1994. *Archives of Pediatric and Adolescent Medicine*, 155, 360–365.

Crook, C.K. (1992). Cultural artefacts in social development: The case of computers. In II. McGurk (Ed.), *Childhood social development: Contemporary perspectives*. Hove, UK: Lawrence Erlbaum.

Crossette, B. (1998). Most consuming more, and the rich much more. *New York Times*, September 13. Retrieved November 15, 2007 from *http://query.nytimes.com/gst/fullpage.html?res=9405E5DB1431F930 A2575AC0A96E958260&sec=&spon=&pagewanted=print*

Crowley, A.E., & Hoyer, W.D. (1994). An integrative framework for understanding two-sided persuasion. *Journal of Consumer Research*, 20, 561–574.

Csikszentmihalyi, M. (2003). *Good business: Leadership, flow, and the making of meaning*. New York: Viking.

Cullingford, C. (1984). *Children and television*. Aldershot, UK: Gower.

Daily Mail (2007). The high street sweatshops: Primark and M&S factories in India pay 13p an hour. Retrieved October 13, 2007 from *http://www.dailymail.co.uk/pages/live/articles/news/news. html?in_article_id=479571&in_page_id=1770*

d'Astous, A. (1990). An inquiry into the compulsive side of normal consumers. *Journal of Consumer Policy*, 113, 15–31.

Datar, A., Sturm, R., & Magnabosco, J.L. (2004). Childhood overweight and academic performance: National study of kindergartners and first-graders. *Obesity Research*, 12, 58–68.

124        *References*

8

124        *References*

Davies, J., Foxall, G.R., & Pallister, J. (2002). Beyond the intention-behaviour mythology: An integrated model of recycling. *Marketing Theory*, 2, 29–113.

Davis, D., & Vernon, M.L. (2002). Sculpting the body beautiful: Attachment style, neuroticism, and use of cosmetic surgeries. *Sex Roles*, 47, 129–138.

Davis, M.H., & Stephan, W.G. (1980). Attributions for exam performance. *Journal of Applied Social Psychology*, 10, 235–248.

Davison, G.C., & Neale, J.M. (1998). *Abnormal psychology* (7th edition). New York: Wiley.

DeAngelis, T. (2005). Cosmetic surgery's dark side. *Monitor on Psychology*, 36, 41.

Deci, E.L., & Ryan, R.M. (1985a). *Intrinsic motivation and self-determination in human behaviour*. New York: Plenum.

Deci, E.L., & Ryan, R.M. (1985b). The general causality orientations scale: Self-determination in personality. *Journal of Research in Personality*, 19, 109–134.

Deci, E.L., & Ryan, R.M. (1987). The support of autonomy and the control of behaviour. *Journal of Personality and Social Psychology*, 53, 1024–1037.

Deitz, T., Ostrom, E., & Stern, P. (2003). The struggle to govern the commons. *Science*, 302, 1907–1912.

DeJong, W., & Kleck, R.E. (1986). The social psychological effects of overweight. In C.P. Herman, M.P. Zanna & E.T. Higgins (Eds.), *Physical appearance, stigma, and social behavior*. Hillsdale, NJ: Lawrence Erlbaum.

Delinsky, S.S. (2005). Cosmetic surgery: A common and accepted form of self-improvement. *Journal of Applied Psychology*, 35, 2012–2028.

Demarest, J., & Allen, R. (2000). Body image: Gender, ethnic and age differences. *Journal of Social Psychology*, 140, 465–472.

Dennison, B., Erb, A., & Jenkins, P. (2002). Television viewing and television in bedroom associated with overweight risk among low-income preschool children. *Pediatrics*, 109, 1028–1035.

De Pelsmacker, P., Driesen, L., & Rayp, G. (2005). Do consumers care about ethics? Willingness to pay for fair-trade coffee. *Journal of Consumer Affairs*, 39, 363–385.

DeSarbo, W.S., & Edwards, E.A. (1996). Typologies of compulsive behaviour: A constrained clusterwise regression approach. *Journal of Consumer Psychology*, 5, 231–262.

Devos-Comby, L., & Salovey, P. (2002). Applying persuasion strategies to alter HIV-relevant thoughts and behaviour. *Review of General Psychology*, 6, 287–304.

Dibb, S., & Harris, L. (1996). *A spoonful of sugar. Television food advertising aimed at children: An international comparative study.* London: Consumers International.

Diener, E., & Biswas-Diener, R. (2002). Will money increase subjective well-being? *Social Indicators Research,* 57, 119–169.

Diener, E., Lucas, R.E., & Napa Scollon, C. (2009). Beyond the hedonic treadmill: Revising the adaption theory of well-being. In E. Diener (Ed.), *The science of well-being: The collected works* (pp. 103–118). New York: Springer Science.

Diener, E., & Seligman, M.E.P. (2002). Very happy people. *Psychological Science,* 13, 81–84.

Dietz, W.H. (1996). The role of lifestyle in health: The epidemiology and consequences of inactivity. *Proceedings of the Nutrition Society,* 55, 829–840.

Dietz, W.H. (2004). Overweight in childhood and adolescence. *New England Journal of Medicine,* 350, 855–857.

Dittmar, H. (1992). *The social psychology of material possessions: To have is to be.* Hemel Hempstead, UK: Harvester Wheatsheaf.

Dittmar, H. (2004). Understanding and diagnosing compulsive buying. In R. Coombs (Ed.), *Handbook of addictive disorders* (pp. 411–450). New York: Wiley.

Dittmar, H. (2008). *Consumer culture, identity and well-being: The search for the 'good life' and the 'body perfect'.* Hove, UK: Psychology Press.

Dittmar, H., & Beattie, J. (1998). Impulsive and excessive buying behaviour. In P. Taylor-Gooby (Ed.), *Choice and public policy: The new welfare consumers* (pp. 123–144). London: Macmillan.

Dittmar, H., & Pepper, L. (1994). To have is to be: Materialism and person perception in working-class and middle-class British adolescents. *Journal of Economic Psychology,* 15, 233–251.

Dominick, J.R., & Greenberg, B.S. (1972). Attitudes toward violence: The interaction of television exposure, family attitudes, and social class. In G.A. Comstock & E.A. Rubenstein (Eds.), *Television and social behaviour: Television and adolescent aggressiveness,* Vol. 3 (pp. 314–335). Washington, DC: Government Printing Office.

Doosje, B., Ellemers, N., & Spears, R. (1999). Commitment and intergroup behaviour. In N. Ellemers, R. Spears, & B. Doosje (Eds.), *Social identity context, commitment, content* (pp. 84–106). Oxford: Blackwell.

Douglas, M., & Isherwood, B. (1979). *The world of goods: Towards an anthropology of consumption.* New York: Basic Books.

Dow, K., & Downing, T.E. (2007). *The atlas of climate change: Mapping the world's greatest challenge.* Berkley: University of California Press.

Drabman, R.S., & Thomas, M.H. (1974). Does media violence increase children's toleration of real-life aggression? *Developmental Psychology*, 10, 418–421.

Drentea, P., & Lavrakas, P.J. (2000). Over the limit: The association among health, race and debt. *Social Science and Medicine*, 50, 517–529.

Du Nann Winter, D. (2003). Shopping for sustainability: Psychological solutions to overconsumption. In T. Kasser & A.D. Kanner (Eds.), *Psychology and consumer culture: The struggle for a good life in a materialistic world*. Washington, DC: American Psychological Association.

Dunlap, R.E., & Van Liere, K.D. (1986). Commitment to the dominant social paradigm and concern for environmental quality. *Social Science Quarterly*, 65, 1013–1028.

Dunn, S. (2000). Global temperature drops. In L.R. Brown, M. Renner & B. Halweil (Eds.), *Vital signs, 2000: The environmental trends that are shaping our future* (pp. 64–65). New York: Norton.

DuRant, R.H., Baranowski, T., Johnson, M., & Thompson, W.O. (1994). The relationship among television watching, physical activity, and body composition of young children. *Pediatrics*, 94, 449–455.

Durkin, K. (1985). *Television, sex roles, and children*. Milton Keynes, UK: Open University Press.

Eagly, A.H., & Chaiken, S. (1975). An attribution analysis of the effect of communicator characteristics on opinion change: The case of communicator attractiveness. *Journal of Personality and Social Psychology*, 32, 136–144.

Ehrlich, P.R., & Ehrlich, A.H. (1990). *Healing the planet*. Reading, MA: Addison Wesley.

Ellaway, A., & Macintyre, S. (2000). Shopping for food in socially contrasting localities. *British Food Journal*, 102, 52–59.

Ellemers, N., De Gilder, D., & Van den Heuvel, H. (1998). Career-oriented versus team-oriented commitment and behavior at work. *Journal of Applied Psychology*, 83, 717–730.

Elliott, K.A., & Freeman, R.B. (2001). *White hats or Don Quixotes? Human rights vigilantes in the global economy*. Cambridge, MA: National Bureau of Economic Research.

Elliott, R. (1994). Compulsive consumption: Function and fragmentation in postmodernity. *Journal of Consumer Policy*, 17, 159–179.

Elliott, R. (1997). Existential consumption and irrational desire. *European Journal of Marketing*, 34, 285–296.

Elliott, R., & Wattanasuwan, K. (1998). Brands as symbolic resources for the construction of identity. *International Journal of Advertising*, 17, 131–144.

Emmons, R.A., Cheung, C., & Tehrani, K. (1998). Assessing spirituality through personal goals: Implications for research on religion and subjective well-being. *Social Indicators Research*, 45, 391–422.

Erikson, E. (1968). *Identity: Youth and crisis*. London: Faber.

Escalas, J.E., & Bettman, J.R. (2003). You are what they eat: The influence of reference groups on consumers' connections to brands. *Journal of Consumer Psychology*, 13, 339–348.

European Commission (2007). Cosmetics and animal tests. Retrieved October 9, 2007 from *http://ec.europa.eu/enterprise/cosmetics/html/cosm_animal_test.htm*

Everett, P.B., Hayward, S.C., & Meyers, A.W. (1974). The effects of a token reinforcement procedure on bus ridership. *Journal of Applied Behavior Analysis*, 7, 1–9.

Faber, R.J. (2003). Self-control and compulsive buying. In T. Kasser & A.D. Kanner (Eds.), *Psychology and consumer culture: The struggle for a good life in a materialistic world*. Washington, DC: American Psychological Association.

Faber, R.J., & O'Guinn, T.C. (1992). A clinical screener for compulsive buying. *Journal of Consumer Research*, 19, 459–469.

Faber, R.J., O'Guinn, T.C., & Krych, R. (1987). Compulsive consumption. In M. Wallendorf & P. Anderson (Eds.), *Advances in consumer research* (pp. 132–135). Provo, UT: Association for Consumer Research.

Falkner, N.H., Neumark-Sztainer, D., Story, M., Jeffery, R.W., Beuhring, T., & Resnick, M.D. (2001). Social, educational, and psychological correlates of weight status in adolescents. *Obesity Research*, 9, 32–42.

Farr, R.M. (1996). *The roots of modern social psychology: 1872–1954*. Oxford: Blackwell.

Fazio, R.H., & Zanna, M.P. (1978). Attitudinal qualities relating to the strength of the attitude-behavior relationship. *Journal of Experimental Social Psychology*, 14, 398–408.

Feingold, A. (1992). Good looking people are not what we think. *Psychological Bulletin*, 111, 304–341.

Feingold, A., & Mazzella, R. (1998). Gender differences in body image are increasing. *Psychological Science*, 9, 190–195.

Feng, J., Spence, I., & Pratt, J. (2007). Playing an action video game reduces gender differences in spatial cognition. *Psychological Science*, 18, 850–855.

Ferguson, C.J. (2010a). Introduction to the special issue on video games. *Review of General Psychology*, 14, 66–67.

Ferguson, C.J. (2010b). Blazing angels or resident evil? Can violent video games be a force for good? *Review of General Psychology*, 14, 68–81.

Ferguson, C.J. (2010c). Genetic contributions to antisocial personality and behavior (APB): A meta-analytic review from an evolutionary perspective. *Journal of Social Psychology*, 150, 160–180.

Ferguson, C.J., Cruz, A., & Rueda, S. (2008). Gender, video game playing habits and visual memory tasks. *Sex Roles: A Journal of Research*, 58, 279–286.

Festinger, L. (1954). A theory of social comparison processes. *Human Relations*, 7, 117–120.

Festinger, L. (1957). *A theory of cognitive dissonance*. Stanford, CA: Stanford University Press.

Figueroa, A., Downey, S., Sieder, J., Lauerman, J., Pierce, E., & Roberts, E. (2000). Our quest to be perfect. *Newsweek*, August 9. Retrieved July 8, 2000 from *http://web2infotrac.galegroup.com/itw/in*

Firat, A.F., & Venkatesh, A. (1995). Liberatory postmodernism and the reenchantment of consumption. *Journal of Consumer Research*, 22, 239–267.

Fiske, J. (1989). *Understanding popular culture*. London: Routledge.

Fiske, A., Kitayama, S., Markus, H., & Nisbett, R. (1998). The cultural matrix of social psychology. In D. Gilbert, S. Fiske & G. Lindzey (Eds.), *Handbook of social psychology*. New York: McGraw-Hill.

Flavell, J.H., Flavell, E.R., Green, F.L., & Korfmacher, J.E. (1990). Do young children think of television images as pictures or real objects? *Journal of Broadcasting and Electronic Media*, 34, 399–419.

Flavin, C., & Dunn, S. (1999). Responding to the threat of climate change. In L.R. Brown, C. Flavin & F. French (Eds.), *State of the world, 1999: A Worldwatch Institute report on progress toward a sustainable society* (pp. 113–130). New York: Norton.

Fletcher, A. (2006). Marks & Spencer dives into ethical consumer market. Retrieved March 28, 2009 from *http://www.foodnavigator.com/Financial-Industry/Marks-Spencer-dives-into-ethical-consumer-market*

Flynn, J.R. (1994). IQ gains over time. In R. J. Sternberg (Ed.), *The encyclopaedia of human intelligence* (pp. 617–623). New York: Macmillan.

Folkes, V.S., & Kamins, M.A. (1999). Effects of information about firms' ethical and unethical actions on consumers' attitudes. *Journal of Consumer Psychology*, 8, 243–259.

Food and Agriculture Organization of the United Nations (2006). State of food insecurity in the world 2006. Retrieved November 13, 2007 from *ftp://ftp.fao.org/docrep/fao/009/a0750e/a0750e00.pdf*

FoodQuality News (2003). Antibiotics uncovered. Retrieved September 3, 2007 from *http://www.foodqualitynews.com/news/ng.asp?id=13303-antibiotics-uncovered*

Foreyt, J.P., & Goodrick, G.D. (1995). The ultimate triumph of obesity. *Lancet*, 346, 134–135.

Foster, J.D., Shrira, I., & Campbell, W.K. (2006). Theoretical models of narcissism, sexuality and relationship commitment. *Journal of Social and Personal Relationships*, 23, 367–386.

Fraj, E., & Martinez, E. (2006). Environmental values and lifestyles as determining factors of ecological consumer behaviour: An empirical analysis. *Journal of Consumer Marketing*, 23, 133–144.

Franklin, J., Denyer, G., Steinbeck, K.S., Caterson, I.D., & Hill, A.J. (2006). Obesity and risk of low self-esteem: A statewide survey of Australian children. *Pediatrics*, 118, 2481–2487.

Frederickson, B.L., & Roberts, T. (1997). Objectification theory: Toward understanding women's lived experiences and mental health risks. *Psychology of Women Quarterly*, 21, 173–206.

Fredrickson, B.L., Roberts, T.A., Noll, S.M., Quinn, D.M., & Twenge, J.M. (1998). That swimsuit becomes you: Sex differences in self-objectification, restrained eating, and math performance. *Journal of Personality and Social Psychology*, 75, 269–284.

French, S.A., Jeffery, R.W., Story, M., Hannan, P., & Snyder, M.P. (1997). A pricing strategy to promote low-fat snack choices through vending machines. *American Journal of Public Health*, 87, 849–851.

Friends of the Earth (2004). Scandal, whitewash, cover-up. Retrieved October 14, 2007 from *http://www.foe.co.uk/resource/reports/palm_oil_summary.pdf*

Fromm, E. (1976). *To have or to be?* New York: Harper Row.

Fukukawa, K. (2003). A theoretical review of business and consumer ethics research: Normative and descriptive approaches. *Marketing Review*, 3, 381–401.

Gaines, L., & Esserman, J. (1981). A quantitative study of young children's comprehension of television programs and commercials. In J.F. Esserman (Ed.), *Television advertising and children: Issues, research and findings*. New York: Child Research Service.

Gamlin, J., Romo, P.D., & Hesketh, T. (2007). Exposure of young children working on Mexican tobacco plantations to organophosphorous and carbamic pesticides, indicated by cholinesterase depression. *Child: Care, Health and Development*, 33, 246–248.

Garcés, L. (2002). *The detrimental impacts of industrial animal agriculture*. A report for Compassion in World Farming Trust. Retrieved February 12, 2009 from *http://www.ciwf.org.uk/includes/documents/cm_docs/2008/d/detrimental_impact_industrial_animal_agriculture_2002.pdf*

Gardner, B.B., & Levy, S.J. (1955). The product and the brand. *Harvard Business Review*, 33, 33–39.

Gardner, G.T., & Stern, P.C. (1996). *Environmental problems and human behaviour*. Needham Heights, MA: Allyn & Bacon.

Gare, S. (1999). The beauty beast. *Weekend Australian Chronicles of the Future*, November 27–28, p. 10.

Garner, D.M. (1997). The 1997 body image survey results. *Psychology Today*, 30, 30–44, 75–80.

Gaugnano, G., Stern, P.C., & Dietz, T. (1995). Influences on attitude-behavior relationships: A natural experiment with curbside recycling. *Environment and Behavior*, 27, 699–718.

Gauntlett, D. (1995). *Moving experiences: Understanding television's influences and effects*. Luton, UK: John Libbey.

Gentile, D.A. (2009). Pathological video game use among youth 8 to 18: A national study. *Psychological Science*, 20, 594–602.

Geographical (2008). March issue. Royal Geographical Society, UK.

Gerbner, G. (1972). Violence in television drama: Trends and symbolic functions. In G.A. Comstock and E.A. Rubenstein (Eds.), *Television and social behavior*, Vol. 1 (pp. 28–187). Media Content and Control. Washington, DC: US Government Printing Office.

Gibbins, K., & Schneider, A. (1980). Meaning of garments: Relation between impression of an outfit and the message carried by its component garments. *Perceptual and Motor Skills*, 51, 287–291.

Gilbert, D.T., Giesler, R.B., & Morris, K.A. (1995). When comparisons arise. *Journal of Personality and Social Psychology*, 69, 227–236.

Glanz, K., Basil, M., Maibach, E., Goldberg, J., & Snyder, D. (1998). Why Americans eat what they do: Taste, nutrition, cost, convenience, and weight control concerns as influences on food consumption. *Journal of American Diet Association*, 98, 1118–1126.

Glick, D., Keene-Osborn, S., Gegax, T.T., Bai, M., Clemetson, L., Gordon, D., et al. (1999). Anatomy of a massacre. *Newsweek*, May 3, p. 24.

Gold, M. (2004). *The global benefits of eating less meat*. A report for Compassion in World Farming Trust. Retrieved January 10, 2008 from *http://www.ciwf.org/publications/reports/The_Global_Benefits_of_Eating_Less_Meat.pdf*

Goldberg, M.E., Gorn, G.J., Peracchio, L.A., & Bamossy, G. (2003). Understanding materialism among youth. *Journal of Consumer Psychology*, 13, 278–288.

Goldsmith, T., & McElroy, S.L. (2000). Compulsive buying: Associated disorders and drug treatment. In A.L. Benson (Ed.), *I shop, therefore I am: Compulsive buying and the search for self* (pp. 217–242). New York: Jason Aronson.

Goldstein, J.H. (1994). Sex differences in toy play and use of video games. In J.H. Goldstein (Ed.), *Toys, play and child development*. Cambridge: Cambridge University Press.

Golombok, S., & Hines, M. (2002). Sex differences in social development. In P. Smith & C. Hart (Eds.), *Blackwell handbook of childhood social development* (pp. 117–136). Oxford: Blackwell.

Gonzales, M.H., Aronson, E., & Costanzo, M.A. (1988). Using social cognition and persuasion to promote energy conservation: A quasi-experiment. *Journal of Applied Social Psychology*, 18, 1049–1066.

Gore, A. (2006). *An inconvenient truth: The planetary emergency of global warming and what we can do about it*. New York: Rodale.

Gortmaker, S.L., Must, A., Perrin, J.M., Sobol, A.M., & Dietz, W.H. (1993). Social and economic consequences of overweight in adolescence and young adulthood. *New England Journal of Medicine*, 329, 1008–1012.

Gotesdam, K.G., & Agras, W.S. (1995). General population-based epidemiological survey of eating disorders in Norway. *International Journal of Eating Disorders*, 18, 119–126.

Granö, N., Virtanen, M., Vahtera, J., Elovainio, M., & Kivimäki, M. (2004). Impulsivity as a predictor of smoking and alcohol consumption. *Personality and Individual Differences*, 7, 1693–1700.

Grant, J.E. (2003). Three cases of compulsive buying treated with naltrexone. *International Journal of Psychiatry in Clinical Practice*, 7, 223–225.

Green, C.S., & Bavelier, D. (2003). Action video game modifies visual selective attention. *Nature*, 423, 534–537.

Green, C.S., & Bavelier, D. (2007). Action video game experience alters the spatial resolution of vision. *Psychological Science*, 18, 88–94.

Greenberg, B.S., Fazel, S., & Weber, M. (1986). *Children's view on advertising*. New York: Independent Broadcasting Authority.

Greenberg, B.S., Sherry, J., Lachlan, K., Lucas, K., & Holmstrom, A. (2008). Orientations to video games among gender and age groups. *Simulation and Gaming*. Advance online publication. doi:10.1177/1046878108319930.

Greenfield, P.M. (1984). *Mind and the media: The effects of television, video games and computers*. Aylesbury, UK: Fontana.

Greenfield, P.M. (1998). The cultural evolution of IQ. In U. Neisser (Ed.), *The rising curve: Long-term gains in IQ and related measures* (pp. 81–123). Washington, DC: American Psychological Association.

Greenfield, P., Brannon, C., & Lohr, D. (1994). Two-dimensional representation of movement through three-dimensional space: The role of video game expertise. *Journal of Applied Developmental Psychology*, 15, 87–104.

Greer, D., Potts, R., Wright, J., & Huston, A. (1982). The effects of television commercial form and commercial placement on children's social behavior and attention. *Child Development*, 53, 611–619.

Griffiths, M.D. (1997). Friendship and social development in children and adolescents: The impact of electronic technology. *Educational and Child Psychology*, 14, 25–27.

Grimes, T., Anderson, J., & Bergen, L. (2008). *Media violence and aggression: Science and ideology*. Thousand Oaks, CA: Sage.

Grinde, B. (2005). Darwinian happiness: Can the evolutionary perspective on well-being help us improve society? *World Futures: The Journal of General Evolution*, 61, 317–329.

Groesz, L.M., Levine, M.P., & Murnen, S.K. (2002). The effect of experimental presentation of thin media images on body dissatisfaction: A meta-analytic review. *International Journal of Eating Disorders*, 31, 1–16.

Grogan, S. (1999). *Body image: Understanding body dissatisfaction in men, women and children.* London: Routledge.

Grubb, E.L., & Hupp, G. (1968). Perception of self, generalized stereotypes, and brand selection. *Journal of Marketing Research*, 5, 58–63.

Grube, J.W., Weir, I.L., Getslaf, S., & Rokeach, M. (1984). Own value system, value images, and cigarette smoking. *Personality and Social Psychology Bulletin*, 10, 306–313.

Grunert, S.C., & Juhl, H.J. (1995). Values, environmental attitudes, and buying of organic foods. *Journal of Economic Psychology*, 16, 39–62.

Gunter, B., & Harrison, J. (1997). Violence in children's programmes on British television. *Children and Society*, 11, 143–156.

Gunter, B., Oates, C., & Blades, M. (2005). *Advertising to children on TV.* Mahwah, NJ: Lawrence Erlbaum.

Halliwell, E., & Dittmar, H. (2004). Does size matter? The impact of model's body size on women's body-focused anxiety and advertising effectiveness. *Journal of Social and Clinical Psychology*, 23, 104–122.

Hardin, G. (1968). The tragedy of the commons. *Science*, 162, 1243–1248.

Hardin, G. (1993). *Living within limits: Ecology, economics and population taboos.* Oxford: Oxford University Press.

Harris, D., & Carr, A. (2001). Prevalence of concern about physical appearance in the general population. *British Journal of Plastic Surgery*, 54, 223–226.

Harris, J. (2001). The effects of computer games on young children: A review of the research. RDS occasional paper 72. London: Home Office.

Harrison, K. (2000). The body electric: Thin-ideal media and eating disorders in adolescents. *Journal of Communication*, 50, 119–143.

Hart, D., & Damon, W. (1986). Developmental trends in self-understanding. *Social Cognition*, 4, 388–407.

Harter, S. (2003). The development of self-representations during childhood and adolescence. In M.R. Leary & J.P. Tangney (Eds.), *Handbook of self and identity* (pp. 610–642). New York: Guilford Press.

Hatcher, S. (1994). Debt and deliberate self-poisoning. *British Journal of Psychiatry*, 164, 111–114.

Hatoum, I.D., & Belle, D. (2004). Mags and abs: Media consumption and bodily concerns in men. *Sex Roles*, 51, 397–407.

Hearold, S. (1986). A synthesis of 1043 effects of television on social behavior. In G. Comstock (Ed.), *Public communications and behaviour*, Vol. 1 (pp. 65–133). New York: Academic Press.

Heinberg, L.H., & Thompson, J.K. (1995). Body image and televised images of thinness and attractiveness: A controlled laboratory investigation. *Journal of Social and Clinical Psychology*, 14, 325–338.

Hekkert, M.P., van den Reek, J., Worrell, E., & Turkenburg, W.C. (2002). The impact of material efficient end-use technologies on paper use and carbon emissions. *Resources, Conservation and Recycling*, 36, 241–266.

Helgeson, J.G., & Supphellen, M. (2004). A conceptual and measurement comparison of self-congruity and brand personality. *International Journal of Market Research*, 46, 205–233.

Henard, D.H. (2002). Negative publicity: What companies need to know about public relations. *Public Relations Quarterly*, 47, 8–12.

Henderson, J.A., Coveney, J.D., Ward, P.R., & Taylor, A. (2009). Governing childhood obesity: Framing regulation of fast food advertising in the Australian print media. *Social Science and Medicine*, 69, 1402–1408.

Henderson-King, D., & Brooks, K.D. (2009). Materialism, sociocultural appearance messages, and paternal attitudes predict college women's attitudes about cosmetic surgery. *Psychology of Women Quarterly*, 33, 133–142.

Henderson-King, D., & Henderson-King, E. (2005). Acceptance of cosmetic surgery: Scale development and validation. *Body Image*, 2, 137–149.

Henderson-King, D., & Henderson-King, E. (2008). *Self-objectification, self-consciousness, and appearance-related variables as predictors of cosmetic surgery attitudes.* Manuscript submitted for publication.

Herman, E.S., & Chomsky, N. (1988). *Manufacturing consent: The political economy of mass media.* New York: Pantheon.

Hickman, M. (2010). Sting in the tail of the Royal Mail deal: More junk mail. *Independent*, March 10, pp. 4–5.

Higgins, E.T. (1987). Self-discrepancy: A theory relating self and affect. *Psychological Review*, 94, 319–340.

Higgins, E.T. (1989). Self-discrepancy theory: What patterns of self-beliefs cause people to suffer? In L. Berkowitz (Ed.), *Advances in experimental social psychology*, Vol. 22 (pp. 93–136). New York: Academic Press.

Higgins, E.T. (1999). Self-discrepancy: A theory relating self and affect. In R.F. Baumeister (Ed.), *The self in social psychology* (pp. 150–181). Philadelphia, PA: Psychology Press.

Higgins, E.T., Klein, R., & Strauman, T. (1987). Self-discrepancies: Distinguishing among self-states, self-state conflicts, and emotional vulnerabilities. In K.M. Yardley & T.M. Honess (Eds.), *Self and identity: Psychosocial perspectives* (pp. 173–186). New York: Wiley.

134                                  References

Hines, J.M., Hungerford, H.R., & Tomera, A.N. (1986). Analysis and
    synthesis of research on responsible environmental behavior: A meta-
    analysis. *Journal of Environmental Education*, 18, 1–8.
Hogg, M.A., & Vaughan, G.M. (2005). *Social psychology* (4th edition).
    Harlow, UK: Pearson.
Hogg, M.A., & Williams, K.D. (2000). From I to we: Social identity and
    the collective self. *Group Dynamics: Theory, Research, and Practice*,
    4, 81–97.
Holbrook, M.B. (1992). Patterns, personalities, and complex relation-
    ships in the effects of self on mundane everyday consumption: These are
    495 of my most and least favorite things. In J.F. Sherry & B. Sternthal
    (Eds.), *Advances in Consumer Research*, Vol. 19 (pp. 417–423). Provo,
    UT: Association for Consumer Research.
Holbrook, M.B., & Hirschman, E.C. (1982). The experiential aspects
    of consumption: Fantasies, feelings and fun. *Journal of Consumer
    Research*, 9, 132–140.
Holland, J.J. (2000). Groups link media to child violence. July 25.
    Retrieved November 4, 2007 from *http://www.ap.org*
Hollander, E. (Ed.) (1993). *Obsessive-compulsive related disorders*.
    Washington, DC: American Psychiatric Press.
Holloway, S.L., & Valentine, G. (2000). Corked hats and *Coronation
    Street*: British and New Zealand children's imaginative geographies of
    the other. *Childhood*, 7, 335–357.
Holt, D.B. (1995). How consumers consume: A typology of consumption
    practices. *Journal of Consumer Research*, 22, 1–16.
Honigman, R.J., Phillips, K.A., & Castle, D.J. (2004). A review of psy-
    chosocial outcomes for patients seeking cosmetic surgery. *Plastic and
    Reconstructive Surgery*, 113, 1229–1237.
Horgen, K.B., Choate, M., & Brownell, K. (2001). Television food adver-
    tising: Targeting children in a toxic environment. In D.G. Singer &
    J.L. Singer (Eds.), *Handbook of children and the media* (pp. 447–462).
    Thousand Oaks, CA: Sage.
Hovland, C.I., & Weiss, W. (1951). The influence of source credibil-
    ity on communication effectiveness. *Public Opinion Quarterly*, 15,
    635–650.
Hsu, L.K.G. (1994). *Eating disorders*. New York: Guilford Press.
Huston, A.C., & Wright, J.C. (1998). Mass media and children's develop-
    ment. In W. Damon (Gen. Ed), *Handbook of child psychology*, Vol. 4.
    *Child psychology in practice* (pp. 999–1058). New York: Wiley.
Ikeuchi, H., Fujihara, T., & Dohi, I. (2000). Involuntary loss of the
    extended self: Survey results of the loss of important possessions
    by great earthquake. *Japanese Journal of Social Psychology*, 16,
    27–38.

Ince, P.J. (1994). *Recycling and long-range timber outlook.* General technical report RM-242. Fort Collins, CO: USDA Forest Service, Rocky Mountain Forest and Range Experiment Station.

In Defense of Animals (2007). Cosmetic testing. Retrieved September 10, 2007 from *http://www.idausa.org/facts/costesting.html*

Information Centre (2006). Statistics on obesity, physical activity and diet: England, 2006. Retrieved January 12, 2008 from *http://www.ic.nhs. uk/webfiles/publications/opan06/OPAN%20bulletin%20finalv2.pdf*

Ingram, R., Skinner, S., & Taylor, V. (2005). Consumers' evaluation of unethical marketing behaviors: The role of customer commitment. *Journal of Business Ethics*, 62, 237–252.

International Labour Organisation (2007a). Child labour. Retrieved October 5, 2007 from *http://www.ilo.org/global/Themes/Child_Labour/lang--en/index.htm*

International Labour Organisation (2007b). Out of sight: Girls in mining. Retrieved October 5, 2007 from *http://www.ilo.org/global/About_the_ILO/Media_and_public_information/Feature_stories/lang--en/WCMS_084034/index.htm*

Islam, F. (2006). Child labour making Tesco clothes. Retrieved February 5, 2010 from *http://www.channel4.com/news/articles/business_money/child%20labour%20making%20tesco%20clothes/170400*

Isler, L., Popper, E., & Ward, S. (1987). Children's purchase requests and parental responses: Results from a diary study. *Journal of Advertising Research*, 27, 28–39.

Ito, M., & Bittani, M. (2009). Gaming. In M. Ito, S. Baumer, M. Bittani, D. Boyd, R. Cody, B. Herr-Stephenson et al. (Eds.), *Hanging out, messing around, geeking out: Living and learning with new media* (pp. 195–242). Cambridge, MA: MIT Press.

Iverson, R.D., & Erwin, P.J. (1997). Predicting occupational injury: The role of negative affectivity. *Journal of Occupational and Organizational Psychology*, 70, 113–128.

Jackson Harris, R. (2004). *A cognitive psychology of mass communication.* Hillsdale, NJ: Lawrence Erlbaum.

Jacobson, M.F., & Brownell, K.D. (2000). Small taxes on soft drinks and snack foods to promote health. *American Journal of Public Health*, 90, 854–857.

Jaglom, L.M., & Gardner, H. (1981). The preschool television viewer as anthropologist. In H. Kelly & H. Gardner (Eds.), *New directions in child development: Viewing children through television* (pp. 9–30). San Francisco, CA: Jossey-Bass.

Jain, S.P., & Posavac, S.S. (2001). Prepurchase attribute verifiability, source credibility, and persuasion. *Journal of Consumer Psychology*, 11, 169–180.

Jason, L.A., & Hanaway, L. (1997). *Remote control: A sensible approach to kids, TV, and the new electronic media.* Sarasota, FL: Professional Resource Press.

Jeffrey, D.B., McLellarn, R.W., & Fox, D.T. (1982). The development of children's eating habits: The role of television commercials. *Health Education Quarterly, 9,* 174–189.

Jepson, P., Jarvie, J.K., MacKinnon, K., & Monk, K.A. (2001). The end for Indonesia's lowland forests? *Science, 292,* 859–861.

Joergens, C. (2006). Ethical fashion: Myth or future trend? *Journal of Fashion Marketing and Management, 10,* 360–371.

Jones, D.C., & Crawford, J.K. (2006). The peer appearance culture during adolescence: Gender and body mass variations. *Journal of Youth and Adolescence, 35,* 257–269.

Josselson, R. (1994). The theory of identity development and the question of intervention. In S. Archer (Ed.), *Interventions for adolescent identity development* (pp. 12–25). Thousand Oaks, CA: Sage.

Jung, K., & Lee, W. (2006). Cross-gender brand extensions: Effects of gender of the brand, gender of consumer, and product type on evaluation of cross-gender extensions. *Advances in Consumer Research, 33,* 67–74.

Kahle, L.R., Beatty, S.E., & Homer, P. (1986). Alternative measurement approaches to consumer values: The list of values (LOV) and values and life style (VALS). *Journal of Consumer Research, 13,* 405–409.

Kalodner, C.R. (1997). Media influences on male and female non-eating-disordered college students: A significant issue. *Eating Disorders, 5,* 47–57.

Kanner, A.D., & Soule, R.G. (2003). Globalization, corporate culture, and freedom. In T. Kasser & A.D. Kanner (Eds.), *Psychology and consumer culture: The struggle for a good life in a materialistic world* (pp. 49–670). Washington, DC: American Psychological Association.

Karno, M., & Golding, J.M. (1991). Obsessive-compulsive disorder. In L.N. Robinson & D.A. Regier (Eds.), *Psychiatric disorders in America.* New York: Free Press.

Kashdan, T.B., & Breen, W.E. (2007). Materialism and diminished well-being: Experiential avoidance as a mediating mechanism. *Journal of Social and Clinical Psychology, 26,* 521–539.

Kasser, T. (2002). *The high price of materialism.* Cambridge, MA: MIT Press.

Kasser, T., & Ryan, R.M. (1993). A dark side of the American dream: Correlates of financial success as a central life aspiration. *Journal of Personality and Social Psychology, 65,* 410–422.

Kasser, T., & Ryan, R.M. (1996). Further examining the American dream: Differential correlates of intrinsic and extrinsic goals. *Personality and Social Psychology Bulletin, 22,* 280–287.

Kasser, T., & Ryan, R.M. (2001). Be careful what you wish for: Optimal functioning and the relative attainment of intrinsic and extrinsic goals. In P. Schmuck & K.M. Sheldon (Eds.), *Life goals and well-being: Towards a positive psychology of human striving* (pp. 116–131). Göttingen, Germany: Hogrefe & Huber.

Kasser, T., Ryan, R.M., Couchman, C.E., & Sheldon, K.M. (2003). Materialistic values: Their causes and consequences. In T. Kasser & A.D. Kanner (Eds.), *Psychology and consumer culture: The struggle for a good life in a materialistic world* (pp. 49–670). Washington, DC: American Psychological Association.

Kasser, T., Ryan, R.M., Zax, M., & Sameroff, A.J. (1995). The relations of maternal and social environments to late adolescents' materialistic and prosocial values. *Developmental Psychology*, 31, 907–914.

Kasser, T., & Sheldon, K.M. (2002). What makes for a merry Christmas? *Journal of Happiness Studies*, 3, 313–329.

Keat, R. (1991). Consumer sovereignty and the integrity of practices. In R. Keat & N. Abercrombie (Eds.), *Enterprise culture* (pp. 216–230). London: Routledge.

Kempton, W., Darley, J.M., & Stern, P.C. (1992). Psychological research for the new energy problems: Strategies and opportunities. *American Psychologist*, 47, 1213–1223.

Kennedy, S.H., & Garfinkel, P.E. (1992). Advances in the diagnosis and treatment of anorexia nervosa and bulimia nervosa. *Canadian Journal of Psychiatry*, 37, 309–315.

Kernan, J.B., & Sommers, M.S. (1967). Meaning, value and the theory of promotion. *Journal of Communication*, 17, 109–135.

Keski-Rahkonen, A., Hoek, H.W., Susser, E.S., Linna, M.S., Sihvola, E., Raevouri, A., et al. (2007). Epidemiology and course of anorexia nervosa in the community. *American Journal of Psychiatry*, 164, 1259–1265.

Kessler, E.-M., Rakoczy, K., & Staudinger, U.M. (2004). The portrayal of older people in prime time TV series: The match with gerontological evidence. *Ageing and Society*, 24, 531–552.

Kids Health (2005). Overweight and obesity. Retrieved October 10, 2007 from*http://www.kidshealth.org/parent/general/body/overweight_obesity.html*

Kilmartin, C.T. (2000). *The masculine self* (2nd edition). Boston, MA: McGraw-Hill.

Kim, Y., Kasser, T., & Lee, H. (2003). Self-concept, aspirations, and well-being in South Korea and the United States. *Journal of Social Psychology*, 143, 277–290.

Kingdom, J. (1992). *There's no such thing as society? Individualism and community.* Milton Keynes, UK: Open University Press.

Klein, N. (1999). *No logo: Money, marketing, and the growing anti-corporate movement.* New York: Picador and St. Martin's Press.

Kleine, R.E., III, Kleine, S., & Kernan, J.B. (1993). Mundane consumption and the self: A social-identity perspective. *Journal of Consumer Psychology, 2,* 209–235.

Koestner, R., Bernieri, F., & Zuckerman, M. (1992). Self-regulation and consistency between attitudes, traits and behaviours. *Personality and Social Psychology Bulletin, 18,* 52–59.

Kohlberg, L. (1981). *The philosophy of moral development: Moral stages and the idea of justice.* New York: Harper & Row.

Kohut, H., & Wolf, E.S. (1978). The disorders of the self and their treatment: An outline. *International Journal of Psychoanalysis, 59,* 413–425.

Koolstra, C.M., van der Voort, T.H.A., & van der Kamp, L.J. (1997). Television's impact on children's reading comprehension and decoding skills: A 3-year panel study. *Reading Research Quarterly, 32,* 128–152.

Koran, L.M., Faber, R.J., Aboujaoude, E., Large, M.D., & Serpe, R.T. (2006). Estimated prevalence of compulsive buying behaviour in the United States. *American Journal of Psychiatry, 163,* 1806–1812.

Korten, D.C. (1995). *When corporations rule the world.* West Hartford, CT: Berrett-Koehler.

Kosowski, T.R., McCarthy, C., Reavey, P.L., Scott, A.M., Wilkins, E.G., Cano, S.J., Klassen, A.F., Carr, N., Cordeiro, P.G., & Pusic, A.L. (2009). A systematic review of patient-reported outcome measures after facial cosmetic surgery and/or nonsurgical facial rejuvenation. *Plastic Reconstructive Surgery, 123,* 1819–1827.

Kottler, J., Montgomery, M., & Shepard, D. (2003). Acquisitive desire: Assessment and treatment. In T. Kasser & A.D. Kanner (Eds.), *Psychology and consumer culture: The struggle for a good life in a materialistic world.* Washington, DC: American Psychological Association.

Kottler, J.A., & Stevens, H. (1999). Interventions. In J.A. Kottler (Ed.), *Exploring and treating acquisitive desire: Living in the material world* (pp. 103–111). Thousand Oaks, CA: Sage.

Kotz, K., & Story, M. (1994). Food advertisements during children's Saturday morning television programming: Are they consistent with dietary recommendations? *Journal of the American Dietetic Association, 94,* 1296–1300.

Kraepelin, E. (1915). *Psychiatrie* (8th edition). Leipzig: Johann Ambrosius Barth.

Krauss, R.M., Freedman, J.L., & Whitcup, M. (1978). Field and laboratory studies of littering. *Journal of Experimental Social Psychology, 14,* 109–122.

Krohmer, H., Lucia, M., & Bettina, N. (2006). The interaction between a brand's personality and its consumers: Performance implications and implementation issues. Paper presented at the 35th EMAC Conference, Athens, Greece.

Krosnik, J.A., & Abelson, R.P. (1992). The case for measuring attitude strength in surveys. In J. Tanur (Ed.), *Questions about questions* (pp. 177–203). New York: Russell Sage Foundation.

Kubey, R. (1986). Television use in everyday life: Coping with unstructured time. *Journal of Communication*, 36, 108–123.

Kumanyika, S. (1993). Ethnicity and obesity development in children. In C.L. Williams & S.Y.S Kimm (Eds.), *Prevention and treatment of childhood obesity* (pp. 81–92). Annals of the New York Academy of Sciences, Vol. 699. New York: New York Academy of Sciences.

Kumanyika, S.K., & Grier, S. (2006). Targeting interventions for ethnic minority and low-income populations. *Future of Children*, 16, 187–207.

Kunkel, D. (1988). Children and host-selling television commercials. *Communication Research*, 15, 71–92.

Kunkel, D., & Gantz, W. (1992). Children's television advertising in the multi-channel environment. *Journal of Communication*, 42, 134–152.

Kwak, H., Zinkhan, G.M., & Crask, M.R. (2003). Diagnostic screener for compulsive buying: Applications to the USA and South Korea. *Journal of Consumer Affairs*, 37, 161–169.

Lang, T., & Hines, C. (1993). *The new protectionism*. London: Earthscan.

Larson, R. (2001). Commentary. In D.R. Anderson, A.C. Huston, K.L. Schmitt, D.L. Linebarger & J.C. Wright (Eds.), *Early childhood television viewing and adolescent behaviour*. Monographs of the Society for Research in Child Development, 66(1), Serial No. 264.

Larson, R.W., & Verma, S. (1999). How children and adolescents spend time across the world: Work, play, and developmental opportunities. *Psychological Bulletin*, 125, 701–736.

Lawrence, L. (1990). The psychodynamics of the compulsive female shopper. *American Journal of Psychoanalysis*, 50, 67–70.

Lazarus, R.S. (1991). *Emotion and adaptation*. New York: Oxford University Press.

Lee, J. (2005). Real women warm to 'real' ads. *The Age*, October 3. Retrieved November 3, 2007 from *http://www.theage.com.au/news/fashion/real-women-warm-to-real-ads/2005/10/02/1128191610142.html*

Lehman, P. (1993). *Running scared: Masculinity and the representation of the male body*. Philadelphia: Temple University Press.

Lejoyeux, M., Hourtané, M., & Adés, J. (1995). Compulsive buying and depression. *Journal of Clinical Psychiatry*, 56, 38.

Lejoyeyx, M., Tassian, V., Solomon, J., & Adés, J. (1997). Study of compulsive buying in depressed patients. *Journal of Clinical Psychiatry*, 58, 169–173.

Leonard-Barton, D. (1981). The diffusion of active-residential solar energy equipment in California. In A. Shama (Ed.), *Marketing solar energy innovations* (pp. 243–257). New York: Praeger.

Lever, J., Frederick, D.A., & Peplau, L.A. (2006). Does size matter? Men's and women's views on penis size across the lifespan. *Psychology of Men and Masculinity*, 7, 129–143.

Levine, J.M. (1999). Solomon Asch's legacy for group research. *Personality and Social Psychology Review*, 3, 358–364.

Levine, M.P., & Smolak, L. (1992). Toward a developmental model of the psychopathology of eating disorders: The example of early adolescence. In J.H. Crowther, S.E. Hobfoll, D.L. Tennenbaum & M.A.P. Stephens (Eds.), *The etiology of bulimia nervosa: The individual and family context* (pp. 59–80). Washington, DC: Hemisphere.

Levy, S.J. (1959). Symbols for sale. *Harvard Business Review*, 37, 117–124.

Lewis, M. (1990). Self-knowledge and social development in early life. In L. Pervin (Ed.), *Handbook of personality: Theory and research* (pp. 277–300). New York: Guilford Press.

Liebert, D., Sprafkin, J., Liebert, R., & Rubinstein, E. (1977). Effects of television commercial disclaimers on the product expectations of children. *Journal of Communication*, 27, 118–124.

Lievers, S., Serra, P., & Watson, J. (1986). Religion and visiting hospitalized old people: Sex differences. *Psychological Reports*, 58, 705–796.

Livesley, W.J., & Bromley, D.B. (1973). *Person perception in childhood and adolescence*. New York: Wiley.

Lloyd-Kolkin, D. (1982). Teaching students to become critical television viewers. *Learning, Media and Technology*, 8, 99–108.

London Paper (2007). Rainforests threatened. May 10, p. 12.

Luhtanen, R.K., & Crocker, J. (2005). Alcohol use in college students: Effects of level of self-esteem, narcissism, and contingencies of self-worth. *Psychology of Addictive Behaviors*, 19, 99–103.

Lunt, P.K., & Livingstone, S.M. (1992). *Mass consumption and personal identity: Everyday economic experience*. Buckingham, UK: Open University Press.

Maccoby, E.E. (1998). *The two sexes: Growing up apart, coming together (The family and public policy)*. Cambridge, MA: Harvard University Press.

Maccoby, E.E. (2000). Perspectives on gender development. *International Journal of Behavioral Development*, 24, 398–406.

Macken, D. (1993). Selling by male. *Sydney Morning Herald Good Weekend Magazine*, April 24, pp. 8–12.

Major, B., Sciacchitano, A., & Crocker, J. (1993). In-group versus out-group comparisons and self-esteem. *Personality and Social Psychology Bulletin*, 19, 711–721.

Mares, M., & Woodard, E.H. (2001). Prosocial effects on children's social interactions. In D.G. Singer & J.L. Singer (Eds.), *Handbook of children and the media* (pp. 183–205). Thousand Oaks, CA: Sage.

Markey, P.M., & Markey, C.N. (2010). Vulnerability to violent video games: A review and integration of personality research. *Review of General Psychology*, 2, 82–91.

Markey, P.M., & Scherer, K. (2009). An examination of psychoticism and motion capture controls as moderators of the effects of violent video games. *Computers in Human Behavior*, 25, 407–411.

Marsh, H.W., Kong, C.-K., & Hau, K.T. (2000). Longitudinal multilevel models of the big-fish-little-pond effect on academic self-concept: Counterbalancing contrast and reflected-glory effects in Hong Kong schools. *Journal of Personality and Social Psychology*, 78, 337–349.

Marshall, T. (2000). Exploring a fiscal food policy: The case of diet and ischaemic heart disease. *British Medical Journal*, 320, 301–305.

Martineau, P. (1957). *Motivation in advertising*. New York: McGraw-Hill.

Maslow, A.H. (1943). A theory of human motivation. *Psychological Review*, 50, 370–396.

Maslow, A.H. (1954). *Motivation and personality*. New York: Harper & Row.

Mattoon, A.T. (2000). Paper piles up. In L.R. Brown, M. Renner & B. Halweil (Eds.), *Vital signs, 2000: The environmental trends that are shaping our future* (pp. 78–79). New York: Norton.

McArdle, H. (2010). Junk food adverts blamed for Scottish children's obesity. *Herald Scotland*, June 14. Retrieved from *http://www.heraldscotland.com/news/health/junk-food-adverts-blamed-for-scottish-children-s-obesity-1.1034634*

McCauley, C., Thangavelu, K., & Rozin, P. (1988). Sex stereotyping of occupations in relation to television representations and census facts. *Basic and Applied Social Psychology*, 9, 197–212.

McCracken, G. (1993). The value of the brand: An anthropological perspective. In D.A. Aaker & A. Biel (Eds.), *Brand Equity and Advertising*. Hillsdale, NJ: Lawrence Erlbaum.

McDougall, D. (2007). Child sweatshop shame threatens Gap's ethical image. *Observer*, October 28, pp. 36–37.

McElroy, S.L., Keck, P.E., & Phillips, K.A. (1995). Kleptomania, compulsive buying, and binge-eating disorder. *Journal of Clinical Psychiatry*, 55, 14–26.

McElroy, S.L., Keck, P.E., Pope, H.G., Jr, Smith, J.M.R., & Strakowski, S.M. (1994). Compulsive buying: A report of 20 cases. *Journal of Clinical Psychiatry*, 55, 242–248.

McKelvie, S.J. (1993). Stereotyping in perception of attractiveness, age, and gender in schematic faces. *Social Behavior and Personality*, 21, 121–128.

McKirnan, D.J. (1980). The conceptualization of deviance: A conceptualization and initial test of a model of social norms. *European Journal of Social Psychology*, 10, 79–93.

McSmith, A. (2006). The rich nations pollute, and the poor nations suffer consequences. *Independent*, March 25, p. 2.

Meilman, P.W. (1979). Cross-sectional age changes in ego identity status during adolescence. *Developmental Psychology*, 15, 230–231.

Mellin, A., Neumark-Sztainer, D., Story, M., Ireland, M., & Resnick, M. (2002). Unhealthy behaviors and psychosocial difficulties among overweight adolescents: The potential impact of familial factors. *Journal of Adolescent Health*, 31, 145–153.

Mellon, M. (2001). Hogging it: Estimates of antimicrobial abuse in livestock. Retrieved October 10, 2007 from *http://www.ucsusa.org/ food_and_environment/antibiotics_and_food/hogging-it-estimates- of-antimicrobial-abuse-in-livestock.html*

Michaelis, L. (2003). Sustainable consumption and greenhouse gas mitigation. *Climate Policy*, 3, 135–146.

Miech, R.A., Kumanyika, S.K., Stettler, N., Link, B.G., Phelan, J.C., & Chang, V.W. (2006). Trends in the association of poverty with overweight among us adolescents, 1971–2004. *Journal of the American Medical Association*, 295, 2385–2393.

Mieszkowska, N., Sims, D., & Hawkins, S. (2007). *Fishing, climate change and north-east Atlantic cod stocks.* Retrieved January 10, 2010 from *http://www.wwf.org.uk/filelibrary/pdf/cc_cod_report.pdf*

Miller, D.T., & Prentice, D.A. (1996). The construction of social norms and standards. In E.T. Higgins & A.W. Kruglanski (Eds.), *Social psychology: Handbook of basic principles* (pp. 799–829). New York: Guilford Press.

Mintel (1994). *The green consumer.* Special report. London: Author.

Mitchell, J.A., Redlin, J., Wonderlich, S., Crosby, R., Faber, R., Miltenberger, R., et al. (2002). The relationship between compulsive buying and eating disorders. *International Journal of Eating Disorders*, 32, 107–111.

Mitchell, J.E., Burgard, M., Faber, R., Crosby, R.D., & de Zwaan, M. (2006). Cognitive behavioural therapy for compulsive buying disorder. *Behavior Research and Therapy*, 44, 1859–1865.

Mitchell, T.R., Thompson, L., Peterson, E., & Cronk, R. (1997). Temporal adjustment in the evaluation of events: The 'rosy view'. *Journal of Experimental Social Psychology*, 33, 421–448.

Montague, C.T., Farooqi, I.S., Whitehead, J.P., Soos, M.A., Rau, H., Wareham, N.J., et al. (1997). Congenital leptin deficiency is associated with severe early-onset obesity in humans. *Nature*, 387, 903–908.

Montemayor, R., & Eisen, M. (1977). The development of self-conceptions from childhood to adolescence. *Developmental Psychology*, 13, 314–319.

Moore, M.E., Stunkard, A., & Srole, L. (1962). Obesity, social class, and mental illness. *Journal of the American Medical Association*, 181, 138–142.

Morf, C.C., & Rhodewalt, F. (2001). Unravelling the paradoxes of narcissism: A dynamic self-regulatory processing model. *Psychological Inquiry*, 12, 177–196.

Morton, H. (1990). Television food advertising: A challenge for the new public health in Australia. *Community Health Studies*, 14, 153–161.

Morwitz, V.G., Steckel, J., & Gupta, A. (2007).When do purchase intentions predict sales? *International Journal of Forecasting*, 23, 347–364.

Mowen, J.C., & Spears, N. (1999). Understanding compulsive buying among college students: A hierarchical approach. *Journal of Consumer Psychology*, 8, 407–430.

Mudur, G. (1995). Monsoon shrinks with aerosol models. *Science*, 270, 1922.

Mueller, A., Mueller, U., Albert, P., Mertens, C., Silbermann, A., Mitchel, J.E., et al. (2007). Hoarding in a compulsive buying sample. *Behaviour Research and Therapy*, 45, 2754–2763.

Munson, J.M., & Spivey, W.A. (1980). Assessing self-concept. In J.C. Olson (Ed.), *Advances in consumer research*, Vol. 7 (pp. 598–603). Ann Arbor, MI: Association for Consumer Research.

Myers, D.G. (1993). *The pursuit of happiness: Who is happy and why*. New York: Morrow.

Myers, D.G. (2000). The funds, friends, and faith of happy people. *American Psychologist*, 55, 56–57.

Nail, P.R., McDonald, G., & Levy, D.A. (2000). Proposal of a four-dimensional model of social response. *Psychological Bulletin*, 126, 454–470.

Nastasi, B.K., & Clements, D.H. (1993). Motivational and social outcomes of cooperative computer education environments. *Journal of Educational Computing Research*, 4, 15–43.

Nastasi, B.K., & Clements, D.H. (1994). Effectance motivation, perceived scholastic competence, and higher-order thinking in two cooperative computer environments. *Journal of Educational Computing Research*, 10, 249–275.

National Center for Health Statistics (1999). Prevalence of overweight among children and adolescents. Retrieved May 20, 2005 from *http://www.cdc.gov/nchs/products/pubs/pubd/hestats/overwght99.htm*

Nesse, R.M., & Williams, G.C. (1994). *Why we get sick*. New York: New York Times Books.

Nestle, M., & Jacobson, M.F. (2000). Halting the obesity epidemic: A public health policy approach. *Public Health Reports*, 115, 12–24.

New Economics Foundation (2005). Retrieved February 16, 2006 from *http://www.neweconomics.org/gen/z_sys_PublicationDetail. aspx?PID=172*

Newson, E. (1994). Video violence and the protection of children. *Journal of Mental Health*, 3, 221–226.

New South Wales Health Care Complaints Commission (1999). Cosmetic Surgery Inquiry transcript, April 12. Strawberry Hills, Australia: Author.

NHS (2006). Statistics on obesity, physical activity and diet: England, 2006. Retrieved August 12, 2007 from *http://www.ic.nhs.uk/webfiles/ publications/opan06/OPAN%20bulletin%20finalv2.pdf*

Niedenthal, P.M., Cantor, N., & Kihlstrom, J.F. (1985). Self to prototype matching: A strategy for social decision-making. *Journal of Personality and Social Psychology*, 48, 575–584.

Noppa, H., & Bengtsson, C. (1980). Obesity in relation to socioeconomic status. A population study of women in Göteborg, Sweden. *Journal of Epidemiology and Community Health*, 34, 139–142.

O'Brien, K.S., Hunter, J., Halberstadt, J., & Anderson, J. (2007). Body image and explicit and implicit anti-fat attitudes: The mediating role of physical appearance comparisons. *Body Image*, 4, 249–256.

Ofcom (2007). Ofcom research identifies changing nature of children's programming. Retrieved November 3, 2007 from *http://www.ofcom. org.uk/media/news/2007/10/nr_20071003*

O'Guinn, T.C., & Faber, R.J. (1989). Compulsive buying: A phenomenological exploration. *Journal of Consumer Research*, 16, 147–157.

Okagaki, L., & Frensch, P.A. (1994). Effects of video game playing on measures of spatial performance: Gender effects in late adolescence. *Journal of Applied Developmental Psychology*, 15, 33–58.

Olli, E., Grendstad, G., & Wollebauk, D. (2001). Correlates of environmental behaviours: Bringing back social context. *Environment and Behavior*, 33, 181–208.

Olson, C.K., Kutner, L.A., & Warner, D.E. (2008). The role of violent video game content in adolescent development: Boys' perspectives. *Journal of Adolescent Research*, 23, 55–75.

Olson, C.K., Kutner, L.A., Warner, D.E., Almerigi, J.B., Baer, L., Nicholi, A.M., II, & Beresin, E.V. (2007). Factors correlated with violent video game use by adolescent boys and girls. *Journal of Adolescent Health*, 41, 77–83.

Oskamp, S. (2000). Psychology for a sustainable society. *American Psychologist*, 55, 496–508.

Ottersen, G., & Sundby, S. (1995). Effects of temperature, wind and spawning stock biomass on recruitment of Arcto-Norwegian cod. *Fisheries Oceanography*, 4, 278–292.

Overlan, L. (1996). 'Overweight' girls at risk. *Newton Tab*, July 2, p. 15.

Owens, J., Maxim, R., McGuinn, M., Nobile, C., Msall, M., & Alario, A. (1999). Television-viewing habits and sleep disturbance in school children. *Pediatrics*, 104, e27.

Oxfam Campaigns (1996). Fair-trade action update. Oxfam internal newsletter. Oxford: Oxfam.

Ozcaglar-Toulouse, N., Shiu, E., & Shaw, D.S. (2006) In search of fair trade: Ethical consumer decision making in France. *International Journal of Consumer Studies*, 30, 502–514.

Paavonen, E.J., Pennonen, M., Roine, M., Valkonen, S., & Lahikainen, A.R. (2006). TV exposure associated with sleep disturbances in 5- to 6-year-old children. *Journal of Sleep Research*, 15, 154–161.

Park, L.E., DiRaddo, A.-M., & Calogero, R.M. (2009). Sociocultural influence and appearance-based rejection sensitivity among college students. *Psychology of Women Quarterly*, 33, 108–119.

Park, S.E., Yun, G.W., McSweeney, J.H., & Gunther, A.C. (2007). Do third-person perceptions of media influence contribute to pluralistic ignorance on the norm of ideal female thinness? *Sex Roles*, 57, 569–578.

Parry, M., Canziani, O., & Palutikof, J. (2008). Key IPCC conclusions on climate change impacts and adaptations. *WMO Bulletin*, 57, 78–85.

Pearce, M.J., Boergers, J., & Prinstein, M.J. (2002). Adolescent obesity, overt and relational peer victimization, and romantic relationships. *Obesity Research*, 10, 386–393.

Pedersen, E.L., & Markee, N.L. (1991). Fashion dolls: Representations of ideals of beauty. *Perceptual and Motor Skills*, 73, 93–94.

Pellegrini, A.D. (2003). Perceptions and functions of play and real fighting in early adolescence. *Child Development*, 74, 1522–1533.

Petty, R.E., & Cacioppo, J.T. (1986). The elaboration likelihood model of persuasion. *Advances in Experimental Social Psychology*, 19, 123–205.

Petty, R.E., Wegener, D.T., & Fabrigar, L.R. (1997). Attitudes and attitude change. *Annual Review of Psychology*, 48, 609–647.

Piaget, J. (1948). *The moral judgement of the child*. Glencoe, IL: Free Press.

Pitta, D.A., Fung, H.-G., & Isberg, S. (1999). Ethical issues across cultures: Managing the differing perspectives of China and the USA. *Journal of Consumer Marketing*, 16, 240–256.

Platt, J. (1973). Social traps. *American Psychologist*, 28, 641–651.

Pope, H.G., Olivardia, R., Gruber, A., & Borowiecki, J. (1999). Evolving ideals of male body image as seen through action toys. *International Journal of Eating Disorders*, 26, 65–72.

Porritt, J. (2004). Foreword. In M. Gold, *The global benefits of eating less meat*. A report for Compassion in World Farming Trust. Retrieved January 10, 2008 from *http://www.ciwf.org/publications/reports/The_Global_Benefits_of_Eating_Less_Meat.pdf*

146     *References*

Postman, N. (1985). *Amusing ourselves to death*. New York: Viking Penguin.

Potter, W.J. (1998). *Media literacy*. Thousand Oaks, CA: Sage.

Poulter, S. (2006). Bargain retailers Tesco's, Asda and Primark depend on sweatshops: Report. Retrieved October 12, 2007 from *http://www.dailymail.co.uk/pages/live/articles/news/news.html?in_article_id=421227&in_page_id=1770*

Powers, R.B., Osborne, J.G., & Anderson, E.G. (1973). Positive reinforcement of litter removal in the natural environment. *Journal of Applied Behavior Analysis, 6*, 579–586.

Prelinger, E. (1959). Extension and structure of the self. *Journal of Psychology, 47*, 13–23.

Pretty, J. (2002). *Agri-culture: Reconnecting people, land and nature*. London: Earthscan.

Price, R.A. (2002). Genetics and common obesities: Background, current status, strategies and future prospects. In T.A. Wadden & A.J. Stunkard (Eds.), *Handbook of obesity treatment* (pp. 73–94). New York: Guilford Press.

Pridmore, S., & Turnier-Shea, Y. (2001). Cosmetic surgery can alter the mental state findings. *Comprehensive Psychiatry, 41*, 696–697.

Pruzinsky, T., & Edgerton, M.T. (Eds.) (1990). *Body-image change in cosmetic plastic surgery*. New York: Guilford Press.

Puhl, R.M., & Brownell, K.D. (2001). Bias, discrimination, and obesity. *Obesity Research, 9*, 788–805.

Pusey, M. (2003). *The experience of middle Australia: The dark side of economic reform*. Melbourne: Cambridge University Press.

Putnam, R.D. (2000). *Bowling alone: The collapse and revival of American community*. New York: Simon & Schuster.

Quaiser-Pohl, C., Geiser, C., & Lehmann, W. (2006). The relationship between computer game preference, gender and mental-rotation ability. *Personality and Individual Difference, 40*, 609–619.

Rallapalli, K.C., Vitell, S.J., Wiebe, F.A., & Barnes, J.H. (1994). Consumer ethical beliefs and personality traits: An exploratory analysis. *Journal of Business Ethics, 13*, 487– 495.

Ravaja, N., Tupeinen, M., Saari, T., Puttonen, S., & Keltikangas-Jarvinen, L. (2008). The psychophysiology of James Bond: Phasic emotional responses to violent video game events. *Emotion, 8*, 114–120.

Rawvas, M.Y.A. (2001). Culture, personality, and morality: A typology of international consumers' ethical beliefs. *International Marketing Review, 18*, 188–209.

Rawwas, M.Y.A., & Isakson, H.R. (2000). Ethics of tomorrow's business managers: The influence of personal beliefs and values, individual characteristics, and situational factors. *Journal of Education for Business, 75*, 321–330.

Ray, J.W., & Klesges, R.C. (1993). Influences on the eating behaviour of children. In C.L. Williams & S.Y.S. Kimm (Eds.), *Prevention and treatment of childhood obesity* (pp. 57–69). *Annals of the New York Academy of Sciences*, Vol. 699. New York: New York Academy of Sciences.

Recycling Consortium (2007). Christmas waste. Retrieved December 18, 2007 from *http://www.recyclingconsortium.org.uk/schools/christmas_waste.htm*

Reidpath, D.D., Burns, C., Garrard, J., Mahoney, M., & Townsend, M. (2002). An ecological study of the relationship between social and environmental determinants of obesity. *Health and Place*, 8, 141–145.

Reingen, P.H., Foster, B.L., Brown, J.J., & Seidman, S.B. (1984). Brand congruence in interpersonal relations: A social network analysis. *Journal of Consumer Research*, 11, 771–783.

Reiter, S.M., & Samuel, W. (1980). Littering as a function of prior litter and the presence or absence of prohibitive signs. *Journal of Applied Social Psychology*, 10, 45–55.

Reuters (2007). Uganda forest faces bulldozers, species at risk. Retrieved June 10, 2007 from *http://www.reuters.com/article/latestCrisis/idUSL04491539*

Rice, M.L., Huston, A.C., Truglio, R.T., & Wright, J.C. (1990). Words from *Sesame Street*: Learning vocabulary while viewing. *Developmental Psychology*, 26, 421–428.

Richins, M.L. (1991). Social comparison and the idealized images of advertising. *Journal of Consumer Research*, 18, 71–83.

Richins, M.L. (1994). Special possessions and the expression of material values. *Journal of Consumer Research*, 21, 522–533.

Richins, M.L., & Dawson, S. (1992). A consumer values orientation for materialism and its measurement: Scale development and validation. *Journal of Consumer Research*, 19, 303–316.

Riddy, P. (2000). Addictive shopping as a form of family communication. In A. Baker (Ed.), *Serious shopping: Psychotherapy and consumerism* (pp. 154–182). London: Free Association Books.

Rindfleisch, A., Burroughs, J.E., & Denton, F. (1997). Family structure, materialism, and compulsive consumption. *Journal of Consumer Research*, 23, 312–325.

Robbins, J. (2001). *The food revolution*. Berkeley, CA: Conari.

Roberts, D.F., Foehr, U.G., & Rideout, V.J. (2005). *Generation M: Media in the lives of 8–18 year-olds*. Menlo Park, CA: Kaiser Family Foundation. Retrieved April 5, 2007 from *http://www. kff.org/entmedia/loader.cfm?url=/commonspot/security/getfile. cfm&PageID=51809*

Roberts, D.F., Foehr, U.G., Rideout, V.J., & Brodie, M. (1999). *Kids and the media @ the new millennium*. Menlo Park, CA: Kaiser Family Foundation.

Roberts, J.A., Tanner, J.F., Jr, & Manolis, C. (2005). Materialism and the family structure and family stress relation. *Journal of Consumer Psychology*, 15, 183–190.

Robinson, M.K., Cohen, C., de Fraissinette, A.B., Ponec, M., Whittle, E., & Fentem, J.H. (2002). Non-animal testing strategies for assessment of the skin corrosion and skin irritation potential of ingredients and finished products. *Food and Chemical Toxicology*, 40, 573–592.

Rodriguez, C. (1998). Even in middle school, girls are thinking thin. *Boston Globe*, November 27, pp. B1, B9.

Rogers, C. (1963). The actualizing tendency in relation to 'motives' and to consciousness. In M.R. Jones (Ed.), *Nebraska symposium on motivation*, Vol. 11 (pp. 1–24). Lincoln: University of Nebraska Press.

Rokeach, M. (1973). *The nature of human values*. New York: Free Press.

Rose, G.M., Shoham, A., Kahle, L.R., & Batra, R. (2006). Social values, conformity, and dress. *Journal of Applied Social Psychology*, 24, 1501–1519.

Rose, P. (2007). Mediators of the association between narcissism and compulsive buying: The roles of materialism and compulsive control. *Psychology of Addictive Behaviors*, 21, 576–581.

Rosser, B.S. (1991). The effects of using fear in public AIDS education on the behaviour of homosexually active men. *Journal of Psychology and Human Sexuality*, 4, 123–134.

Rosser, J., Lynch, P., Caddihy, L., Gentile, D., Klonsky, J., & Merrell, R. (2007). The impact of video games on training surgeons in the 21st century. *Archives of Surgery*, 142, 181–186.

Rule, B.G., & Ferguson, T.J. (1986). The effects of media violence on attitudes, emotions, and cognitions. *Journal of Social Issues*, 42, 29–50.

Ryan, R.M., & Connell, J.P. (1989). Perceived locus of causality and internalization. *Journal of Personality and Social Psychology*, 57, 749–761.

Safir, M.P., Flaisher-Kellner, S., & Rosenmann, A. (2005). When gender differences surpass cultural difference in personal satisfaction with body shape in Israeli college students. *Sex Roles: A Journal of Research*, 52, 369–379.

Sanstad, A.H., & Howarth, R.B. (1994). 'Normal' markets, market imperfections, and energy efficiency. *Energy Policy*, 22, 811–818.

Sarwer, D.B., Cash, T.F., Magee, L., Williams, E.F., Thompson, J.K., Roehrig, M., et al. (2005). Female college students and cosmetic surgery: An investigation of experiences, attitudes, and body image. *Plastic and Reconstructive Surgery*, 115, 931–938.

Sarwer, D.B., Gibbons, L.M., Magee, L., Baker, J.L., Casas, L.A., Glat, P.M., et al. (2005). A prospective, multi-site investigation of patient satisfaction and psychosocial status following cosmetic surgery. *Aesthetic Surgery Journal*, 25, 263–269.

Sarwer, D.B., LaRossa, D., Bartlett, S.P., Low, D.W., Bucky, L.P., & Whitaker, L.A. (2003). Body image concerns of breast augmentation. *Plastic Reconstructive Surgery*, 112, 83–90.

Sarwer, D.B., & Magee, L. (2006). Physical appearance and society. In D.B. Sarwer, T. Pruzinsky, T.F. Cash, R.M. Goldwyn, J.A. Persing & L.A. Whitaker (Eds.), *The psychology of reconstructive and cosmetic plastic surgery: Clinical, empirical, and ethical perspectives* (pp. 23–36). Philadelphia, PA: Lippincott Williams & Wilkins.

Sarwer, D.B., Magee, L., & Crerand, C.E. (2003). Cosmetic surgery and cosmetic medical treatments. In J.K. Thompson (Ed.), *Handbook of eating disorders and obesity* (pp. 718–737). Hoboken, NJ: Wiley.

Sarwer, D.B., Wadden, T.A., Pertschuk, M.J., & Whitaker, L.A. (1998). Body image dissatisfaction and body dysmorphic disorder in 100 cosmetic surgery patients. *Plastic and Reconstructive Surgery*, 101, 1644–1649.

Saunders, S., & Munro, D. (2000). The construction and validation of a consumer orientation questionnaire (SCOI) designed to measure Fromm's (1955) 'marketing character' in Australia. *Social Behavior and Personality*, 28, 219–240.

Schechter, D. (2000). Eye on the media: Television finds new ways to beam violence at us. *Newsday*, May 10, p. A46.

Scherhorn, G. (1990). The addictive trait in buying behaviour. *Journal of Consumer Policy*, 13, 33–51.

Scherhorn, G., Reisch, L.A., & Raab, G. (1990). Addictive buying in West Germany: An empirical study. *Journal of Consumer Policy*, 13, 355–387.

Schiffman, L.G., Sherman, E., & Long, M.M. (2003). Toward a better understanding of the interplay of personal values and the Internet. *Psychology and Marketing*, 20, 169–186.

Schlenker, B.R. (1980). *Impression management: The self-concept, social identity, and interpersonal relations*. Monterey, CA: Brooks/Cole.

Schlosser, S., Black, D.W., Repertinger, S., & Freet, D. (1994). Compulsive buying: Demography, phenomenology, and comorbidity in 46 subjects. *General Hospital Psychiatry*, 16, 205–212.

Schmuck, P., Kasser, T., & Ryan, R.M. (2000). Intrinsic and extrinsic goals: Their structure and relationship to well-being in German & U.S. college students. *Social Indicators Research*, 50, 225–241.

Schmuck, P., & Vlek, C. (2003). Psychologists can do much to support sustainable development. *European Psychologist*, 8, 66–76.

Schofield, M., Hussain, R., & Loxton, D. (2002). Psychosocial and health behavioural covariates of cosmetic surgery: Women's Health Australia study. *Journal of Health Psychology*, 7, 445–457.

Schooler, D., Kim, J.L., & Sorsoli, K.L. (2000). Setting rules or sitting down: Parental mediation of television consumption and adolescent self-esteem, body image, and sexuality. *Sexuality Research and Social Policy*, 3, 49–62.

Schroeder, J.E., & Dugal, S.S. (1995). Psychological correlates of the materialism construct. *Journal of Social Behavior and Personality*, 10, 243–253.

Schwartz, S.H. (1992). Universals in the content and structure of values: Theoretical advances and empirical tests in 20 countries. In M.P. Zanna (Ed.), *Advances in experimental social psychology*, Vol. 25 (pp. 1–65). Orlando, FL: Academic Press.

Schwartz, S.H., & Howard, J.A. (1982). Helping and cooperation: A self-based motivational model. In V.J. Derlege & J. Gizelack (Eds.), *Cooperation and helping behaviour: Theories and research*. New York: Academic Press.

Science Daily (2007). Eating disorders in adolescents. Retrieved December 2, 2007 from *http://www.sciencedaily.com/releases/2007 /11/071119113857.htm*

Science Daily (2009). Children who view adult-targeted TV may become sexually active earlier in life. Retrieved August 27, 2010 from *http:// www.sciencedaily.com /releases/2009/05/090504105555.htm*

Seager, J. (1993). *Earth follies: Coming to feminist terms with the global environmental crisis*. New York: Routledge.

Secord, P.F. (1968). Consistency theory and self-referrent behaviour. In R.P. Abelson, E. Aronson, W.J. McGuire, T.M. Newcomb, M.J. Rosenberg & P.H. Tannenbaum (Eds.), *Theories of cognitive consistency: A source book* (pp. 349–354). Chicago, IL: Rand McNally.

Setterlund, M.B., & Niedenthal, P.M. (1993). Who am I? Why am I here? Self-esteem, self-clarity, and prototype matching. *Journal of Personality and Social Psychology*, 65, 769–780.

Shaw, D., & Clarke, I. (1999). Belief formation in ethical consumer groups: An exploratory study. *Marketing Intelligence and Planning*, 17, 109–119.

Shaw, D., Grehan, E., Shiu, E., Hassan, L., & Thomson, J. (2005). An explanation of values in ethical consumer decision making. *Journal of Consumer Behaviour*, 4, 185–200.

Shaw, D., & Shiu, E. (2002). An assessment of ethical obligation and self-identity in ethical consumer decision-making: A structural equation modelling approach. *International Journal of Consumer Studies*, 26, 286–293.

Shaw, D., & Shiu, E. (2003). Ethics in consumer choice: A multivariate modeling approach. *European Journal of Marketing*, 37, 1485–1498.

Shaw, D., Shiu, E., & Clarke, I. (2000). The contribution of ethical obligation and self-identity to the theory of planned behaviour: An exploration of ethical consumers. *Journal of Marketing Management*, 16, 879–894.

Sheehan, M.O. (2001). Making better transportation choices. In L.R. Brown, C. Flavin & H. French (Eds.), *State of the world, 2001: A Worldwatch Institute report on progress toward a sustainable society* (pp. 103–122). New York: Norton.

Sheldon, K.M., & Kasser, T. (2001). Getting older, getting better: Personal strivings and psychological maturity across the life span. *Developmental Psychology*, 37, 491–501.

Sheppard, S.R.J. (2005). Landscape visualisation and climate change: The potential for influencing perceptions and behaviour. *Environmental Science and Policy*, 8, 637–654.

Simon, B., Stürmer, S., & Steffens, K. (2000). Helping individuals or group members? The role of individual and collective identification in AIDS-volunteerism. *Personality and Social Psychology Bulletin*, 26, 497–506.

Singer, J.L., Singer, D.G., Desmond, R., Hirsch, B., & Nicol, A. (1998). Family mediation and children's cognition, aggression and comprehension of television: A longitudinal study. *Journal of Applied Developmental Psychology*, 9, 329–347.

Singhapakdi, A., Rawwas, M.Y.A., Marta, J.K., & Ahmed, M.I. (1999). A cross-cultural study of consumer perceptions about marketing ethics. *Journal of Consumer Marketing*, 16, 257–272.

Sirgy, M.J., Lee, D.J., Kosenko, R., Meadow, H.L., Rahtz, D., Cieic, M., et al. (1998). Does television viewership play a role in the perception of quality of life? *Journal of Advertising*, 27, 125–142.

Skafte, D. (1989).The effect of perceived wealth and poverty on adolescents' character judgments. *Journal of Social Psychology*, 129, 93–99.

Skinner, B.F. (1953). *Science and human behavior*. New York: Macmillan.

Smith, C.N. (1987). Consumer boycotts and consumer sovereignty. *European Journal of Marketing*, 21, 7–21.

Smith, N.C. (1990). *Morality and the market: Consumer pressure for corporate accountability*. London: Routledge.

Smith, P.K., Cowie, H., & Blades, M. (2003). *Understanding children's development*. Oxford: Blackwell.

Solberg, E.G., Diener, E., & Robinson, M.D. (2003). Why are materialists less satisfied? In T. Kasser & A.D. Kanner (Eds.), *Psychology and consumer culture: The struggle for a good life in a materialistic world*. Washington, DC: American Psychological Association.

Solomon, M.R. (1983). The role of products as social stimuli: A symbolic interactionism perspective. *Journal of Consumer Research*, 10, 319–329.

Solomon, M.R. (1985). *The psychology of fashion*. Lexington, MA: Lexington Books.

Specker, S., de Zwaan, M., Raymond, N., & Mitchell, J. (1994). Psychopathology in subgroups of obese women with and without binge eating disorder. *Comprehensive Psychiatry*, 25, 185–190.

Sperry, S., Thompson, J.K., Sarwer, D.B., & Cash, T.F. (2009). Cosmetic surgery reality TV viewership: Relations with cosmetic surgery attitudes, body image, and disordered eating. *Annals of Plastic Surgery*, 62, 7–11.

Spitzer, R.L., Yanovski, S.Z., Wadden, T.A., Marcus, M.D., Stunkard, A.J., Devlin, M., et al. (1993). Binge eating disorder: Its further validation in a multisite study. *International Journal of Eating Disorders*, 13, 137–153.

Staats, H. (2003). Understanding proenvironmental attitudes and behaviour: An analysis and review of research based on the theory of planned behaviour. In M. Bonnes, T. Lee & M. Bonaiuto (Eds.), *Psychological theories for environmental issues* (pp. 171–202). Aldershot, UK: Ashgate.

Stein, J. (1986). Why girls as young as 9 fear fat and go on diets to lose weight. *Los Angeles Times*, October 29, pp. 1, 10.

Steiner-Adair, C., & Purcell, A. (1996). Approaches to mainstreaming eating disorders prevention. *Eating Disorders*, 4, 294–309.

Stern, B., & Resnik, A. (1978). Children's understanding of a televised commercial disclaimer. In S. Jain (Ed.), *Research frontiers in marketing: Dialogues and directions* (pp. 332–336). Chicago, IL: American Marketing Association.

Stern, P.C. (2000). Psychology and the science of human-environment interaction. *American Psychologist*, 55, 523–530.

Stern, P.C., Dietz, T., Abel, T., Gaugnano, G.A., & Kalof, L. (1999). A social psychological theory of support for social movements: The case of environmentalism. *Human Ecology Review*, 6, 81–97.

Stice, E., Spangler, D., & Agras, W.S. (2001). Exposure to media-portrayed thin-ideal images adversely affects vulnerable girls: A longitudinal experiment. *Journal of Social and Clinical Psychology*, 20, 270–288.

Stickney, M.I., Miltenberger, R.G., & Wolff, G. (1999). A descriptive analysis of factors contributing to binge eating. *Journal of Behavior Therapy and Experimental Psychiatry*, 30, 177–189.

Stiglitz, J.E. (2008). A new agenda for global warming. In A.S. Edlin, J. Bradford Delong, & J.E. Stiglitz (Eds.), *The economists' voice: Top economists take on today's issues* (pp. 22–27). New York: Columbia University Press.

Stokes, R., & Frederick-Recascino, C. (2003). Women's perceived body image: Relations with personal happiness. *Journal of Women and Aging*, 15, 17–29.

Story, M., Neumark-Sztainer, D., & French, S. (2002). Individual and environmental influences on adolescent eating behaviors. *Journal of the American Dietetic Association*, 102, S40–S51.

Strasburger, V.C. (1992). Children, adolescents, and television. *Pediatrics in Review*, 13, 144–151.

Strasburger, V.C., & Wilson, B.J. (2002). *Children, adolescents, and the media*. Thousand Oaks, CA: Sage.

Strong, C. (1996). Features contributing to the growth of ethical consumerism: A preliminary investigation. *Marketing Intelligence and Planning*, 14, 5–13.

Stunkard, A.J. (2002). Binge eating disorder and the night eating syndrome. In T.A. Wadden & A.J. Stunkard (Eds.), *Handbook of obesity treatment* (pp. 107–121). New York: Guilford Press.

Stutman, S. (1993). An opportunity to prevent violence. Retrieved July 10, 2009 from *http://www.apa.org/divisions/div46/articles/stutman. pdf*

Subrahmanyam, K., Kraut, R.E., Greenfield, P.M., & Gross, E.F. (2001). New forms of electronic media: The impact of interactive games and Internet on cognition, socialization, and behaviour. In D. Singer & J. Singer (Eds.), *Handbook of children and the media*. Thousand Oaks, CA: Sage.

Suls, J.M., & Fletcher, B. (1983). Social comparison in the social and physical sciences: An archival study. *Journal of Personality and Social Psychology*, 44, 575–580.

Suls, J.M., & Wheeler, L. (Eds.) (2000). *Handbook of social comparison: Theory and research*. New York: Kluwer/Plenum.

Sunday Times (2006). Computer kids swamp games addiction clinic. July 23. Retrieved from *http://www.timesonline.co.uk/tol/news/world/ article691460.ece*

Swami, V., Arteche, A., Chamorro-Premuzic, T., Furnham, A., Stieger, S., & Haubner, T., et al. (2008). Looking good: Factors affecting the likelihood of having cosmetic surgery. *European Journal of Plastic Surgery, 30, 211–218.

Swami, V., Chamorro-Premuzic, T., Bridges, S., & Furnham, A. (2008). Acceptance of cosmetic surgery: Personality and individual difference predictors. *Body Image*, 6, 7–13.

Swann, W.B., Jr (1990). To be adored or to be known? The interplay of self-enhancement and self-verification. In E.T. Higgins & R.M. Sorrentino (Eds.), *Handbook of motivation and cognition: Foundations of social behavior*, Vol. 2 (pp. 408–448). New York: Guilford Press.

Szmigin, I., Carrigan, M., & O'Loughlin, D. (2007). Integrating ethical brands into our consumption lives. *Journal of Brand Management*, 14, 396–409.

Tajfel, H. (1981). *Human groups and social categories: Studies in social psychology.* Cambridge: Cambridge University Press.

Tajfel, H., & Turner, J.C. (1979). An integrative theory of intergroup conflict. In W.G. Austin & S. Worchel (Eds.), *The social psychology of intergroup relations* (pp. 33–47). Monterey, CA: Brooks/Cole.

Taras, H.L., Sallis, J.F., Patterson, T.L., Nader, P.R., & Nelson, J.A. (1989). Television's influence on children's diet and physical activity. *Journal of Developmental and Behavioral Pediatrics*, 10, 176–180.

Tarrant, M., North, A.C., Edridge, M.D., Kirk, L.E., Smith, E.A., & Turner, R.E. (2001). Social identity in adolescence. *Journal of Adolescence*, 24, 597–609.

Taylor, C.R., & Stern, B.B. (1997). Asian-Americans: Television advertising and the 'model minority' stereotype. *Journal of Advertising*, 26, 47–61.

Taylor, K. (1999). Rapid climate change. *American Scientist*, 87, 320–327.

Taylor, P. (2007). How global warming is changing maps. Retrieved Febuary 15, 2008 from http://www.metro.co.uk/news/64461-how-global-warming-is-changing-maps

Templer, D.I. (2002). *Is size important?* Pittsburgh, PA: CeShore.

Terry, D.J., & Hogg, M.A. (1996). Group norms and the attitude–behavior relationship: A role for group identification. *Personality and Social Psychology Bulletin*, 22, 776–793.

Thompson, A.R., Kent, G., & Smith, J.A. (2002). Living with vitiligo: Dealing with difference. *British Journal of Health Psychology*, 7, 213–225.

Thorpe, S.J., Ahmed, B., & Steer, K. (2004). Reasons for undergoing cosmetic surgery: A retrospective study. *Sexualities, Evolution and Gender*, 6, 75–96.

Times (2007). Revealed: Topshop clothes made with 'slave labour'. Retrieved September 14, 2007 from *http://women.timesonline.co.uk/tol/life_and_style/women/fashion/article2241665.ece*

Tinsley, B.R. (2002). *How children learn to be healthy.* New York: Cambridge University Press.

Trampe, D., Stapel, D.A., & Siero, F.W. (2007). On models and vases: Body dissatisfaction and social comparison effects. *Journal of Personality and Social Psychology*, 92, 106–118.

Triandis, H.C. (1977). *Interpersonal behaviour.* Monterey, CA: Brooks/Cole.

Troiano, R.P., & Flegal, K.M. (1998). Overweight children and adolescents: Description, epidemiology, and demographics. *Pediatrics*, 101, 497–504.

Tudge, C. (2004). *So shall we reap: What's gone wrong with the world's food – and how to fix it.* London: Penguin.

Turkel, A.R. (1998). All about Barbie: Distortions of a transitional object. *Journal of the American Academy of Psychoanalysis*, 26, 165–177.

US Census Bureau (2007). U.S. and world population clocks: POPClocks. Retrieved January 18, 2007 from *http://www.census.gov/main/www/popclock.html*

US Department of Health and Human Services (2010). Hurricane Katrina. Retrieved March 16, 2010 from *http://www.hhs.gov/disasters/emergency/naturaldisasters/hurricanes/katrina/index.html*

Uusitalo, O., & Oksanen, R.M. (2004). Ethical consumerism: A view from Finland. *International Journal of Consumer Studies*, 28, 214–221.

Van Boven, L. (2005). Experientialism, materialism, and the pursuit of happiness. *Review of General Psychology*, 9, 132–142.

Van Boven, L., & Gilovich, T. (2003). To do or to have? That is the question. *Journal of Personality and Social Psychology*, 85, 1193–1202.

Vandewater, E.A., Bickham, D.S., Lee, J.H., Cummings, H.M., Wartella, E.A., & Rideout, V.J. (2005). When television is always on: Heavy television exposure and young children's development. *American Behaviorial Scientist*, 48, 562–577.

van Driel, M.F., Weijmar Schultz, W.C.M., van de Wiel, H.B.M., & Mensink, H.J.A. (1998). Surgical lengthening of the penis. *British Journal of Urology*, 82, 81–85.

Veenhoven, R. (2003). Hedonism and happiness. *Journal of Happiness Studies*, 4, 437–457.

Veitch, R., & Arkkelin, D. (1995). *Environmental psychology: An interdisciplinary perspective*. Englewood Cliffs, NJ: Prentice Hall.

Velasquez-Manoff, M. (2008). Why your happiness matters to the planet: Surveys and research link true happiness to a smaller footprint on the ecology. *Christian Science Monitor*, July 22.

Vermeir, I., & Verbeke, W. (2006). Sustainable food consumption: Exploring the consumer 'attitude-behavioural intention' gap. *Journal of Agricultural and Environmental Ethics*, 19, 169–194.

Vermeir, I., & Verbeke, W. (2007). Sustainable food consumption among young adults in Belgium: Theory of Planned Behaviour and the role of confidence and values. *Ecological Economics*, 64, 542–553.

Verplanken, B., & Holland, R. (2002). Motivated decision-making: Effects of activation and self-centrality of values on choices and behaviour. *Journal of Personality and Social Psychology*, 82, 434–447.

Wadden, T.A., Brownell, K.D., & Foster, G.D. (2002). Obesity: Responding to the global epidemic. *Journal of Consulting and Clinical Psychology*, 70, 510–525.

Wadden, T.A., Foster, G.D., Letizia, K.A., & Wilk, J.E. (1993). Metabolic, anthropometric, and psychological characteristics of obese binge eaters. *International Journal of Eating Disorders*, 14, 17–25.

Wadden, T.A., Womble, L.G., Stunkard, A.J., & Anderson, D.A. (2002). Psychosocial consequences of obesity and weight loss. In T.A. Wadden & A.J. Stunkard (Eds.), *Handbook of obesity treatment* (pp. 144–169). New York: Guilford Press.

Walker, J.M. (1979). Energy demand behaviour in a master-meter apartment complex: An experimental analysis. *Journal of Applied Psychology*, 64, 190–196.

Wallendorf, M., & Arnould, E.J. (1988). 'My favorite things': A cross-cultural inquiry into object attachment, possessiveness, and social linkage. *Journal of Consumer Research*, 14, 531–547.

Walls, R.T., & Smith, T.S. (1970). Development of preferences for delayed reinforcement in disadvantaged children. *Journal of Educational Psychology*, 62, 118–123.

Walters, E., & Kendler, K.S. (1994). Anorexia nervosa and anorexia-like symptoms in a population based twin sample. *American Journal of Psychiatry*, 152, 62–71.

Walters, E.E., Neale, M.C., Eaves, L.J., Lindon, J., & Heath, A.C. (1992). Bulimia nervosa and major depression: A study of common genetic and environmental factors. *Psychological Medicine*, 22, 617–622.

Wartella, E., & Hunter, L. (1983). Children and the formats of television advertising. In M. Meyer (Ed.), *Children and the formal features of television* (pp. 144–165). Munich: K.G. Saur.

Wattanasuwan, K. (2005). The self and symbolic consumption. *Journal of American Academy of Business*, 6, 179–184.

Weinstein, C.S. (1991). The classroom as a social context for learning. *Annual Review of Psychology*, 42, 493–525.

Wicklund, R.A. (1999). The disappearance of defensiveness via I-D compensation. *Psychological Inquiry*, 10, 254–256.

Wicklund, R.A., & Braun, O.L. (1987). Incompetence and the concern with human categories. *Journal of Personality and Social Psychology*, 53, 373–382.

Wicklund, R.A., & Gollwitzer, P.M. (1982). *Symbolic self-completion*. Hillsdale, NJ: Lawrence Erlbaum.

Wildlife Extra (2007). Ugandan forest spared from scourge of bio-fuel. Retrieved January 8, 2007 from *http://www.wildlifeextra.com/mabira-forest629.html*

Williamson, C.E., Saros, J.E., Vincent, W.F., & Smold, J.P. (2009). Lakes and reservoirs as sentinels, integrators, and regulators of climate change. *Limnology and Oceanography*, 54, 2273–2282.

Wills, T.A. (1981). Downward comparison principles in social psychology. *Psychological Bulletin*, 90, 245–271.

Wise, G.L. (1974). Differential pricing and treatment by new car salesmen: The effect of the prospect's race, sex, and dress. *Journal of Business*, 47, 328–330.

Wiseman, C.V., Gray, J.J., Mosimann, J.E., & Ahrens, A.H. (1992). Cultural expectations of thinness in women: An update. *International Journal of Eating Disorders*, 11, 85–89.

Witt, S.D. (1997). Parental influence on children's socialization to gender roles. *Adolescence*, 32, 253–259.

Wolf, N. (1990). *The beauty myth*. London: Vintage.

Wong, N.Y. (1997). Suppose you own the world and no one knows? Conspicuous consumption, materialism, and self. In M. Brooks & D.J. MacInnis (Eds.), *Advances in Consumer Research*, 24, 107–203.

Wood, J.V. (1989). Theory and research concerning social comparisons of personal attributes. *Psychological Bulletin*, 106, 231–248.

Wood Consumption (2007). Paper consumption. Retrieved November 9, 2007 from *http://www.woodconsumption.org/products/paper.pdf*

World Health Organization (1997). The medical impact of the use of antimicrobials in food animals. Retrieved October 7, 2007 from *http://www. who.int/salmsurv/links/en/GSSMedicaluseImpactAMRsberlin97.pdf*

World Health Organization (1998). *Obesity: Preventing and managing the global epidemic*. Geneva: Author.

World Health Organization (2007). Hazardous child labour. Retrieved September 4, 2007 from *http://www.who.int/occupational_health/topics/childlabour/en/*

Wright, J.C., & Huston, A.C. (1983). A matter of form: Potentials of television for young viewers. *American Psychologist*, 38, 835–843.

Wright, J.C., Huston, A.C., Murphy, K.C., St Peters, M., Pinon, M., Scantlin, R., & Kotler, J. (2001). The relations of early television viewing to school readiness and vocabulary of children from low-income families: The early window project. *Child Development*, 72, 1347–1366.

Wright, R. (2000). Nonzero: The logic of human destiny. New York: Vintage

Wu, C., & Shaffer, D.R. (1987). Susceptibility to persuasive appeals as a function of source credibility and prior experience with the attitude object. *Journal of Personality and Social Psychology*, 52, 677–688.

Wundt, W. (1916). *Elements of folk psychology: Outlines of a psychological history of the development of mankind*. London: Allen & Unwin.

WWF (2007). Are we putting our fish in hot water? Retrieved October 14, 2007 from *http://www.wwf.org.uk/filelibrary/pdf/int_hotfish_ma.pdf*

Yanovski, S.Z. (1993). Binge eating disorder: Current knowledge and future directions. *Obesity Research*, 1, 306–324.

Yanovski, S.Z., Nelson, J.E., Dubbert, B.K., & Spitzer, R.L. (1993). Association of binge eating disorder and psychiatric comorbidity in obese subjects. *American Journal of Psychiatry*, 150, 1472–1479.

Young, M.R., DeSarbo, W.S., & Morwitz, V.G. (1998). The stochastic modeling of purchase intentions and behaviour. *Management Science*, 44, 188–202.

Young, V.L., Nemecek, J.R., & Nemecek, D.A. (1994). The efficacy of breast augmentation: breast size increase, patient satisfaction, and psychological effects. *Plastic and Reconstructive Surgery*, 94, 958–969.

Yurchisin, J., & Johnson, K.P.P. (2004). Compulsive buying behaviour and its relationship to perceived social status associated with buying, materialism, self-esteem, and apparel-product involvement. *Family and Consumer Sciences Research Journal*, 32, 291–314.

Zahavi, A. (1975). Mate selection: A selection for a handicap. *Journal of Theoretical Biology*, 53, 205–214.

Zill, N., Davies, E., & Daly, M. (1994). *Viewing of Sesame Street by preschool children in the United States and its relationship to school readiness*. Rockville, MD: Westat.

# Author Index

162 *Author Index*

*Author Index*

*Author Index*

# Subject Index